Heart of the Storm
The Genesis of the Air Campaign against Iraq

Richard T. Reynolds, Colonel, USAF

Volume one of a two-volume series

Air University Press
Maxwell Air Force Base, Alabama

January 1995

Library of Congress Cataloging-in-Publication Data

Reynolds, Richard T.
     Heart of the storm : the genesis of the air campaign against Iraq / Richard T.
    Reynolds. p. cm.
      "January 1995."
      Includes index.
      1. Persian Gulf War, 1991—Aerial operations. I. Title. DS79.724.U6R49
   1995
        956.704'4248—dc20   94-16836
                                                              CIP

ISBN 1-58566-052-3

First Printing January 1995
Second Printing May 1995
Third Printing August 1996
Fourth Printing December 1999
Fifth Printing August 2001
Sixth Printing July 2002
Seventh Printing February 2003

Disclaimer

Note from the Commander of Air University

My predecessor chartered this two-volume set addressing CINCCENT's Desert Shield/Desert Storm air campaign. The work was the assigned duty for the authors, and it joins the more than 30 publications and articles already distributed by Air University Press on Desert Shield/Desert Storm, as well as many more by other publishers.

When I first read *Heart of the Storm*, I was—and remain—deeply concerned about the way people are characterized by the author. I worry that there was a preconceived notion about who really planned and built the air campaign.

So, I wrote many of the principal people in *Heart of the Storm*, sent them a copy of the manuscript, and asked their opinions. That correspondence is filed with the documentation in the Air Force Historical Research Agency. I must tell you that most of them said there were inaccuracies, words and events taken out of context, a definite bias in favor of Col John Warden and his team, and undocumented flourishing/spicing up in the style of Tom Clancy. While I respect these concerns, I did read the interviews, and I did cross-check the work.

Heart of the Storm is not the Air Force historical accounting of the air campaign in Desert Shield/Desert Storm. That responsibility rests with the Air Force historian, to whom all the documentation has been given.

I do believe, however, that *Heart of the Storm* does indeed have value for people trying to understand the genesis of the air campaign and something about complex decision making. It also begins to lay out in the clear light of day some of the important air power doctrine issues which we must understand as professionals.

Our Air Force is good and sound. I am confident that *Heart of the Storm*, as one perspective, will be read, discussed, and considered along with the many other pieces completed and—eventually—with those yet to be done. It will also be tempered with experience, good judgment, and common sense.

JAY W. KELLEY
Lieutenant General, USAF
Commander
Air University

For Mary,

The wind beneath my wings

To preach the message, to insist upon proclaiming it (whether the time is right or not), to convince, reproach, and encourage, as you teach with all patience. The time will come when people will not listen to sound doctrine, but will follow their own desires and will collect for themselves more and more teachers who will tell them what they are itching to hear. They will turn away from listening to the truth and give their attention to legends.

2 Tim. 4:2–4

Contents

Foreword

Airmen all over the world felt relief and exhilaration as the war in the Gulf reached its dramatic conclusion on 28 February 1991. Many nonairmen, of course, experienced those emotions as well—but for a variety of different reasons. Airmen, long uneasy about the lingering inconclusiveness of past applications of their form of military power, now had what they believed to be an example of air power decisiveness so indisputably successful as to close the case forever.

Within the United States Air Force, among those who thought about the uses of air power, there were two basic groups of airmen. The first—smaller and less influential—held to the views of early air pioneers in their belief that air power was best applied in a comprehensive, unitary way to achieve strategic results. The second—much more dominant—had come to think of air power in its tactical applications as a supportive element of a larger surface (land or maritime) campaign.

Thinking in terms of strategic air campaigns, members of the first group found their inclinations reinforced by Col John Warden's book, *The Air Campaign: Planning for Combat*, published in 1988. Over the years, the second group increasingly concentrated on refining specific mission capabilities (close air support, interdiction, air refueling, etc.) that could be offered to a joint force commander for his allocation decisions. Members of this group rarely thought in terms of comprehensive air campaigns to achieve strategic objectives and indeed generally equated the term *strategic* to Strategic Air Command's long-range bomber force in delivery of nuclear weapons. Both groups found agreement in their love of the airplane and their search for acceptance as equal partners with their older sister services.

In that regard, airmen everywhere stepped forward in late February to receive the congratulations they felt were so richly deserved. Put aside, for the moment at least, was the fact that a hot and often bitter debate had taken place within the Air

Force on the eve of Operation Desert Storm over the very issue of the strategic air campaign and the question of whether air power would be used in that form. Here was a story to be told, a piece of history to be recorded. Just how that story would be told was, to my mind, by no means clear.

In the end, of course, the Gulf War did in fact include a strategic air campaign, and the very least that one could say about it was that by so thoroughly destroying the Iraqis' capability to conduct warfare, it permitted a relatively blood-less war-concluding ground operation by coalition army forces. The most that one could say about the air campaign was that it—in and of itself—won the war.

At Air University (AU), where I was serving at the time as commander, direct involvement in Desert Shield/Storm was about as limited as in any part of the Air Force. We had done some early macroanalyses of air campaign options in the Air Force Wargaming Center; we had excused some students from their studies at Air Command and Staff College to act as observers in various headquarters involved in the war; and—like all commands—we had sent support personnel to augment CENTAF forces in the desert. Otherwise, we were as detached as it was possible to be—that is to say, vitally interested but wholly without responsibility. Our responsibility would begin when the guns fell silent.

Within that overall context and in the heady moment of self-congratulation by airmen, two thoughts occurred to me: (1) the story of the Air Force's development of an air campaign would rapidly become hazy as human memories began to fail—either willfully or through natural erosion—and (2) air power's effect on the outcome of the war would become increasingly controversial as non–Air Force institutions realized that their own resources would likely diminish if airmen's conclusions were accepted.

AU could now begin to use the capabilities of its Airpower Research Institute to record the history of the air campaign as quickly and—above all—as honestly as possible. I knew that if the story were told accurately, it would not always be pretty;

nonetheless, if there were to be any hope of learning valid lessons from the war, future generations had to have access to the truth. To that end, I directed three of my best people—Col Ed Mann, Col Suzanne Gehri, and Col Rich Reynolds—to research and write about the Gulf War air campaign and its implications for the future. The first fruit of that effort, Reynolds's *Heart of the Storm,* provides a candid account of the turbulent birth of the strategic air campaign plan that proved decisive in defeating Iraq. I am pleased with his book, and, while it will certainly produce hot—perhaps even bitter—debate among some of the participants described within its covers, I am convinced the book adds much to the institutional understanding of the Air Force. Additionally, it saves some of us from the fate Hemingway spoke of in his introduction to *Men at War:* "As they get further and further away from a war they have taken part in, all men have a tendency to make it more as they wish it had been rather than how it really was."*

CHARLES G. BOYD
General, USAF
Deputy Commander in Chief,
US European Command

Men at War: The Best War Stories of All Time, ed. Ernest Hemingway (1942; reprint, New York: Wing Books, 1991), xv–xvi.

About the Author

Col Richard T. Reynolds is a 21-year Air Force veteran. He has spent most of that time in fighter operations, with assignments in Europe and the United States. In 1989, after a tour at the Pentagon, Reynolds was selected to attend Harvard University, where he wrote a treatise entitled *What Fighter Pilots' Mothers Never Told Them about Tactical Command and Control—and Certainly Should Have.* Published by Harvard's Center for Information Policy Research, this study still enjoys wide circulation in military and civilian circles. Reynolds joined the College of Aerospace Doctrine, Research, and Education (CADRE) at Maxwell AFB, Alabama, as a military doctrine analyst in the fall of 1990 and completed his work on *Heart of the Storm* in the spring of 1994. Colonel Reynolds is currently assigned to Headquarters, United States European Command in Stuttgart, Germany, as chief of theater plans.

Preface

My goal in writing *Heart of the Storm* was to capture, in words, the process by which a disparate group of people conceived and helped forge the most successful air campaign the world has ever known. Such a book would give current and future generations of airmen the opportunity to see, close up, the enormously complex and intensely personal struggles involved in putting together an air campaign plan for a commander in chief. The big questions in my mind were, How can I do it? and—more importantly—How can I do it right?

The approach I used to "do it right" involved interviewing key individuals in the air campaign planning process at as many levels and locations as money and time allowed. My colleagues and I spent over two years with the interviewees, who talked and gestured their way through the tough questions we posed to them. From this interaction, I gleaned most of the particulars about people, circumstances, and events that flavor the story.

This methodology is not unlike that of a reporter who interviews members of the winning team after a championship game. Because each player has a different perception of what happened—usually colored by his own exploits—the reporter's job is to listen carefully to as many accounts as time and circumstance permit and then piece together the essence of the game. Even a good reporter, however, often fails to record fine details, such as brilliant blocks, head fakes, and so forth. To those participants whose heroics I missed, I offer my sincere apology and the explanation that I was just trying to keep my eyes on the ball.

Two years of interviewing produced over 4,000 pages of transcripts, which constitute the principal source material for this book. Additionally—in an attempt to get as close as possible to the "real story"—I culled the thousands of pages of documents produced before, during, and after the Gulf War. I had much help in this endeavor (see acknowledgments) and met routinely with the historians assigned to Desert Storm research at the Center for Air Force History at Bolling AFB in Washington, D.C., to square my findings with their independent work.

I had some very high-powered help in this endeavor to get as close to the real and true story of the genesis of the air campaign as time and circumstances would allow. Lt Gen Jay W. Kelley, the Air University commander, undertook the task of sending the completed *Heart of the Storm* manuscript to every senior officer mentioned in it, along with the request that they review the book for accuracy. The agreement between General Kelley and me was that if anyone in this group found inaccuracies in the book and provided proof of same, I would correct the errors. No such proof was forthcoming.

What came instead were wide-ranging, almost visceral responses that mirrored the strategic/tactical debates between airmen that General Boyd spoke of in his foreword to this book. Some embraced the work for its honesty and candor while others condemned it for a total lack of those same qualities. Some urged immediate, uncensored publication of the work while others were equally adamant that it never see the light of day. Consequently, General Kelley, a good and decent man who—prior to his arrival at Maxwell Air Force Base—had no knowledge of this enterprise, was now entrusted with the unenviable job of deciding whether or not *Heart of the Storm* would be published by the institutional Air Force. The general found himself in the middle of a Texas-sized dilemma. No matter which way he went on the publication issue, he was certain to displease someone.

I am happy to say that we reached a compromise. *Heart of the Storm* will be published in as-close-to-the-original, uncensored form as the current dictates of Air University taste and style allow. Most of the foul language used by the Desert Shield/Storm participants was edited out. In those rare cases in which a curse remains in the published version of the book, it is because the substitution of "expletive deleted" would have significantly altered the meaning of the text. The reader who simply must have the unvarnished version of what was said need only review the citations, which are on file with the US Air Force Historical Research Agency at Maxwell Air Force Base, Alabama.

Heart of the Storm is by no means a definitive account of the events that led to the Gulf War. It is merely my interpretation of those events, after sifting and balancing them as carefully as I knew how, with the advice and counsel of some of the best and brightest people in the business. I sincerely encourage people who have different views to put their arguments together and publish them as quickly as they can. They will find no quarrel with me. The simple truth is, I wanted to give my fellow airmen a readable, accessible, and provable account of the birth of the Gulf War air campaign plan so these warriors would better understand who they are and why they learn to fly and fight as they do.

RICHARD T. REYNOLDS, Colonel, USAF
Patch Barracks, Stuttgart, Germany
8 December 1994

Acknowledgments

I am leery of acknowledgments but grateful that you, the reader, have taken the time to stop here and look over the names of the people who contributed so much to this work. Perhaps your name, or the name of someone you know, is among them. My greatest concern is that I have unintentionally missed one or two or 10 people who did much to make *Heart of the Storm* a reality. I hope you are not one of them.

The Air Force deserves the first and biggest thank-you for having the courage to let me research, write, and publish *Heart of the Storm*. Long may it continue to serve and protect the United States of America. Although many Air Force people lent their assistance, some very special individuals come to mind. Gen Charles G. Boyd, former commander of Air University (AU) at Maxwell AFB, Alabama, endured countless update briefings on the *Heart of the Storm* project and put the prestige of his office solidly behind it, even though many people said it couldn't or shouldn't be done. His oft-repeated admonishment to "get as close to the truth as you can find it" still rings in my ears.

Maj Gen John B. Sams, former commander of the College of Aerospace Doctrine, Research, and Education (CADRE) at AU, was responsible for bringing *Heart of the Storm*'s initial findings to the attention of senior Air Force leaders. His early support was crucial to the project's success. Brig Gen Ervin C. ("Sandy") Sharpe, Jr., who succeeded General Sams at CADRE, went the extra mile on everything, and his cryptic "YGTBSM" marginalia did much to put the Desert Storm research in perspective. I would gladly serve with him in war or peace—anytime, anywhere.

Dr I. B. Holley, Jr., a retired major general in the Air Force Reserve and professor emeritus at Duke University, deserves enormous credit for his part in making *Heart of the Storm* publishable. He spared neither shoe leather nor advice in his circuitous walks with me from CADRE to the Maxwell Officers' Club, where he scrutinized every word of the evolving manuscript. On many a hot summer's day, onlookers were treated to the sight of this sparingly built, slightly stooped, white-haired scholar darting from the shade of one pine tree to another as he made his way to the club, talking nonstop about what needed to be fixed or removed from the text. I learned much from this senior statesman of military history.

Maj Gen William J. Breckner, Jr., USAF, Retired, a bona fide fighter-pilot warrior and combat veteran, gave generously of his time and talents to make this story worth telling. I couldn't have done it without him.

I owe a great debt to Col Edward C. Mann III and Col Suzanne B. Gehri, my research partners, for their insightful interviews and moral support. No doubt Colonel Mann's volume, *Thunder and Lightning: Desert Storm and the Airpower Debates* (forthcoming), will prove more valuable and lasting than my own.

Former director of CADRE's Airpower Research Institute (ARI), Col (now Professor) Dennis M. Drew is due thanks for succumbing to badgering from me and Ed Mann about the need to do this project in the first place. His successor, Col Robert M. Johnston, inherited a passel of headaches but coped brilliantly with all of them and made the book far better than it would have been without him.

The man most responsible for the polish on my prose is Dr Marvin Bassett. As far as I am concerned, he is the best editor in the business. (Of course, readers should be skeptical about these remarks; after all, he got to edit them along with the rest of the book!) His tiny pencil scrawls all over my drafts have convinced me of his genius and editing artistry. People who have seen my original prose argue that Dr Bassett's accomplishments with *Heart of the Storm* are no less remarkable than those of medieval alchemists, who purportedly made pure gold from the basest of metals. I suspect they're right.

My story also includes a heroine—Mrs Juanita Faye Davis of the Air Force Historical Research Agency (HRA) at Maxwell.

Heart of the Storm would not have been possible without Faye—not my volume or Colonel Mann's. Almost single-handedly, she painstakingly transcribed the hundreds of hours of interviews we recorded on audio cassettes as baseline research for this project. Future generations of researchers will thank her for the text she so diligently produced.

Other HRA people deserve mention for their help. Maj Elizabeth A. Sumpter, a reservist, led this ignorant fighter controller through the maze of historical cataloguing and documentation. Her bosses, Col Elliott V. Converse and Col Richard S. Rauschkolb, were very generous with HRA facilities and gave me and my research associates a secure office space in which to pore over the thousands of documents that were of interest to us.

Members of the Air Force Office of History at Bolling AFB, Washington, D.C., gave freely of their time and talent. In particular, Dr Diane Putney, a senior researcher, was critical to the development of *Heart of the Storm*'s story line. An unselfish, brilliant researcher, she willingly shared her discoveries with me and my colleagues in an attempt to nail down what really happened during the development of the Gulf War air campaign. She has my deepest gratitude and admiration.

I would be remiss if I didn't thank all the Desert Storm participants who allowed us to talk with them and transcribe their stories. Their willingness to discuss what they saw and heard during those critical days will be of infinitely more value to the Air Force and the security of this nation than anything I have written. Among this group are two unique airmen, Col Bernard E. ("Ben") Harvey and Col David A. Deptula. During the buildup and execution of Desert Storm, Harvey took detailed notes on everything that happened around him. His efforts proved critical to my work. Another prodigious notetaker during the war, Deptula shared not only his notes but also his insights and a number of helpful wartime documents. I owe him a debt that is far too large to repay.

Lastly, I wish to thank several other very important members of the institutional Air Force. Second Lt Kurt Konopatzke, a banked* pilot who showed up at my door in the fall of 1993 asking for work, quickly became an integral part of our research team. He is responsible for fleshing out the "What Became of Them?" section, originally suggested by ARI's Dr Jim Titus. Thanks to him and Dr Titus as well. Two other significant contributors to this book were my daughter, Emily, who checked my grammar, and my son, Justin, who came up with the idea for the cover design. Since my wife, Sharon, usually has the last word in everything, I thought it appropriate to thank her at this juncture for her editing support and understanding during this long and difficult endeavor.

All the people I have mentioned in this section are part of the institutional Air Force that I love. I pray that *Heart of the Storm*, however humbly, reflects at least a portion of the promise and greatness I see in all of them. Any errors or omissions in the work, however, are entirely my own.

---

*A recent graduate of undergraduate pilot training who is awaiting assignment to an active flying unit.

Chapter 1

Tue/31 Jul 90/Pentagon/Wash DC

Maj Gen Charles A. May shifted uncomfortably in his seat against the back wall of the lavishly appointed briefing room. He was in the "cheap seats," along with other horse-holder two- and three-star generals and admirals from the different services, each accompanying his respective chief to a meeting in the "tank."* As the Air Force's assistant deputy chief of staff for plans and operations, General May was not normally required to attend these tank sessions, but his immediate boss, Lt Gen Jimmie Adams, was on leave and, consequently, the task fell to him.

Initially, this tank session appeared pretty interesting. Gen H. Norman Schwarzkopf, commander in chief (CINC) of United States Central Command (USCENTCOM),** headquartered at MacDill Air Force Base (AFB), Florida, was at the speaker's podium giving his assessment of the situation on the Kuwaiti border to the service chiefs, Gen Colin Powell—chairman of the Joint Chiefs of Staff (JCS)—and Secretary of Defense (SECDEF) Dick Cheney.[1] According to intelligence sources, within the past 72 hours, Iraqi forces at the direction of Saddam Hussein were gathering along the Iraqi/Kuwaiti border in what looked like offensive combat formations. A few of the hard-liners in the Defense Intelligence Agency (DIA) even went so far as to say that there was little doubt that an attack by Iraq into Kuwait was imminent. Schwarzkopf didn't agree.

General Schwarzkopf told the group that he felt there was only a very slim chance that Saddam Hussein would actually send troops into Kuwait. Most likely, this action was simply a bluff to extort controls on oil prices and forgiveness of debts from the Kuwaiti emir and other Arab leaders. Schwarzkopf went on to say that if the intelligence people were right and Saddam did act, at most he would probably go for the oil fields

---

*Secure area in the Pentagon where highly classified discussions take place among senior officers and civilians.

**Hereinafter referred to as CENTCOM unless it is part of a title (as is the case above).

1

in the north of the country and perhaps Bubiyan Island as well.[2] But certainly not the whole country.

Because he was obliged as CINC of USCENTCOM to discuss what his forces were capable of doing in the unlikely event such an attack occurred, Schwarzkopf outlined a series of options that amounted to little more than sticking a finger in Hussein's eye. They involved using some highly classified Air Force and Navy programs to let Saddam know that there was a price to be paid for going into Kuwait. The general was well aware that he was in no position to confront Saddam's war machine directly. The reason was simple: he had no air, land, or sea forces in place in the region. Even if he wanted to initiate anything—assuming the president, Congress, and the Arab states would allow it—many months would pass before a force large enough to deal with the huge Iraqi war machine could be assembled and brought into theater. It wouldn't be easy—not for anyone.

General May shrugged his shoulders and reached back to scratch an itch that had been bothering him almost since Schwarzkopf started speaking. The room had grown warm from the number of bodies filling it. The general had completed his briefing and was fielding a few polite questions from the service chiefs. None of them were throwing any hardballs today. It was as though by tacit agreement each of the "big boys" knew he had to go through the ritual of reviewing the intelligence information and discussing military options with the responsible theater CINC, but no one with any authority—including General Schwarzkopf—really believed they would do anything with it. As the meeting broke up and the service chiefs mingled and passed papers and briefcases to subordinates, the mood around the table was "Ho hum, thanks for the briefing, Norm. We'll try to attend your retirement next summer."[3] Seven thousand miles away in sand and darkness, Iraqi tankers were fueling for the push into Kuwait. When dawn broke, they would be rolling south.

Fri/3 Aug 90/HQ 9AF/Shaw AFB SC

Heat rising off the runway at Shaw AFB in huge, shimmering waves partially obscured the view of Lt Gen

Charles A. ("Chuck") Horner, Ninth Air Force commander, as he completed final preflight checks in his sleek F-16C Viper. Even though the general's flight suit was already partially soaked through with sweat from his walk-around, Horner was looking forward to flying. It had been a rough night.

He had been awakened at 2:00 A.M. by Col Jim Crigger, his director of operations, who told him the Iraqis had invaded Kuwait. Crigger had brought along an intelligence officer, Col Bill Hubbard, who briefed the general on the details of the attack and the latest status on the fighting. It didn't look good. When Hubbard finished his assessment, a grim-faced General Horner listened while Colonel Crigger outlined the actions he had taken.

An eight-man contingency operations planning staff made up of Ninth Air Force operations and intelligence officers had been formed and was working around the clock in the command-post area. Their immediate focus was on dusting off operation plan (OPLAN) no. 1307 and determining what forces needed to be added to or subtracted from it in order to respond to the current crisis. Col John McBroom, commander of the 1st Tactical Fighter Wing, had been called by Crigger and told not to stop doing "business as usual" but to be prepared for a short-notice deployment of his air-to-air-capable F-15C and D Eagles. When Crigger had concluded, Horner nodded his approval and sent the two men on their way.

General Horner didn't get much sleep after that. He half expected General Schwarzkopf to call during the night, but no call came. When morning arrived with still no word from CENTCOM, Horner decided to press on with his normal routine. He was scheduled to attend an accident investigation board debriefing at Langley AFB, Virginia. General Horner would fly there himself in an F-16C and on the way practice dissimilar air combat tactics (DACT) with four Langley birds in a training area somewhere over the ocean. He was glad for the opportunity to fly—to *do* something. This waiting around for phone calls was not his style at all.

Teak 01 Flight was cleared onto the active runway, and as General Horner gave the signal, both he and his wingman plugged in burners and started their takeoff roll. Despite the enormous thrust generated by both jets, it took a long time and a lot of runway to get airborne in the South Carolina heat. Climbing out, General Horner eased the back pressure off the stick and glanced over at his "wingy." He had to admit he was feeling better already. These guys were the best in the world, and Chuck Horner knew it. If Schwarzkopf wanted him in-theater, he had no qualms about going and taking care of business. No qualms at all.

General Horner's radio crackled to life. It was the air route traffic control center with an urgent message for Teak 01. Could he return to base immediately? Horner knew what it was and asked for a clearance back to Shaw. He was on the ground 10 minutes later. Not long after, he walked into his office with his G suit still attached and placed a secure call to General Schwarzkopf at MacDill. The gist of their short conversation was that Schwarzkopf wanted Horner at MacDill as soon as possible to help the CENTCOM staff prepare a briefing for the president on viable military options in the event Saddam Hussein pressed on through Kuwait and into Saudi Arabia. Specifically, General Schwarzkopf wanted Horner to lend assistance on the "air part."[4] Horner agreed, hung up the phone, gathered a few papers off his desk, and headed back to the flight line.

Fri/3 Aug 90/HQ CENTCOM/MacDill AFB FL

Maj Gen Burt Moore hadn't had time to catch his breath since arriving at MacDill from Washington only two months ago and taking over as the new USCENTCOM director of operations (J-3). From the moment he arrived, he was knee-deep in exercises and contingency operations. Before yesterday's invasion of Kuwait, most of the Air Force general's waking hours had been devoted to Internal Look, a CENTCOM-wide command and control (C[2]) procedures exercise that focused on the defense of Saudi Arabia against a large aggressor force. Schwarzkopf had been adamant that the entire CENTCOM staff get on board that exercise.

Thousands of man-hours had been spent fine-tuning the war plan that went along with Internal Look. However, as the exercise started in the last week of July, the plan's time-phased force deployment data (TPFDD)—the document that determined how, why, and when forces and materiel would be brought into theater—remained incomplete. At first, this didn't cause any real problems because, after all, in a C^2 procedures exercise, the sending of troops, bombs, and bullets could all be simulated. However, as actual events in the last days of July began to bear an uncanny resemblance to those in the scenario, General Moore and the rest of the CENTCOM staff began to get a little worried.

And now, things were fast coming to a head at CENTCOM. The whole morning had been spent frantically reviewing war plans and trying to come up with some deployment options for General Schwarzkopf to take with him to Washington for his briefing with President George Bush. Moore had gotten his guidance from Maj Gen Bob Johnston, the newly hired USCENTCOM chief of staff. Because he had been there less time than Moore, Johnston—who had just called—was anxious about everything.

"J-3, this is the chief of staff. What have you got?"

"Bob," replied General Moore, tweaking the Marine Corps general a little bit for his stiff formality, "we are just working on it. You gave me the guidance 45 minutes ago."

There was a slight pause on the other end of the phone. "I think we ought to go in and show the CINC what we've got."

Moore replied, more perplexed than irritated, "I don't have anything!"

General Johnston ignored the comment and continued pressing Moore for an immediate meeting with the CINC. "Well, we need to get some spin on this. We need to make sure we are on the right track."

Burt Moore moved the phone away from his left ear and stared at it for a moment before switching the receiver to his other ear. "Bob," he said slowly, almost soothingly, "we can do that, but what we've got is going to be in pencil. It's not going to look like anything."

"That doesn't matter," said Johnston, a slight edge of confidence and authority returning to his voice as he realized the J-3 was apparently willing, if pressed hard enough, to roll over on this one. "Let's go on up there."[5]

The two men met in Schwarzkopf's outer office several minutes later. General Moore showed Johnston the rough, hand-scrawled figures that his planners—Tom Sewell, Clint Williams, and others—had pulled out of OPLAN nos. 1002-90 and 1307. Their numbers represented a first-shot attempt at trying to determine what forces—in what mixture and in what order—should be sent into theater. As Moore and Johnston discussed the merits of what had been written, Schwarzkopf's exec motioned to them that the general was ready to see them. Moore quickly shoved his note papers inside a manila folder and walked behind Johnston into Schwarzkopf's inner sanctum. It didn't take long for the men to explain what had been accomplished to General Schwarzkopf. He was not impressed.

"What kind of junk is that?"[6] bellowed Schwarzkopf and threw both men out of his office, telling them to come back when they had their act together. This process was repeated several times during the day with the same results. General Moore would go into the office with General Johnston, show the CINC the latest iteration of a deployment plan, and promptly get both men tossed out on their ears.

By early afternoon, General Horner had arrived at MacDill. He went directly to the CINC's office for a quick meeting with General Schwarzkopf to bring him up to speed on what US Air Forces, Central Command (CENTAF) was doing. He then excused himself and went down to the joint operations center (JOC) but didn't stay long. The place was hectic, crowded, and full of tension. Reports and messages were coming in every few minutes, and action officers were scurrying to get them routed to the proper directorates for action. It was not a very good place to think.

Horner made his way through the cipher-locked doors and out into the narrow, tiled hallways. The interior of the building, with its sea-green passageways and low ceilings, looked like the inside of an old Navy warship. It even smelled like one. This was in sharp contrast to the modern, futuristic, and clean outer facade—almost as though two separate architects, with no knowledge or care of what the other was doing, set about designing the inside and outside of the building, never dreaming they were working on the same structure.

General Horner found the back staircase, ambled up the steps—trailing his hand along the paint-flecked rail—turned right, and settled in a small room set aside for visiting dignitaries. At least it was quiet here. He picked up a yellow pad from among the supplies neatly arranged on the desk and began writing. Horner remained there the rest of the afternoon, trying to put to paper his thoughts on how air power could best be used to help solve the crisis in the Middle East.[7]

Around 1800 that evening, General Horner joined General Schwarzkopf in the CINC's private conference room to listen to the staff propose options and courses of action. Meanwhile, General Moore paced nervously outside, waiting his turn to go in and brief the boss—one more time. When the call came, Moore picked up his charts, slipped his dark blue Magic Marker in his pocket, and walked quickly into the conference room.

Horner was seated next to Schwarzkopf and looked up impassively as Moore walked over to the CINC. They had greeted one another in the hall several hours earlier, when General Moore was dashing from room to room trying to collect information on deployments and beddown. Horner hadn't seen him since—until now. Moore walked past General Horner and laid the set of 8" x 11" charts directly in front of Schwarzkopf. He leaned over the table and began to speak: "Sir, we will deploy 24 F-15s with a support package of something less than a squadron of Wild Weasels."

General Schwarzkopf stopped him before he could get to the chart's next bullet and fired back impatiently, "What do you mean with this '24 F-15s'?"

"Well, if you will let me walk you through it here. . . ." Moore moved uncomfortably to Schwarzkopf's other side and continued with his briefing, showing a basic beddown of 24 A-10s, 24 F-16s, and the appropriate number of KC-10 and KC-135 tankers needed to get the fighters across the pond.

"I don't understand that," said Schwarzkopf, gesturing toward the chart. "That's too complicated. I want something simple." Moore started to speak, but before he could complete his sentence, Schwarzkopf interrupted him again, repeating—more ominously this time—"I don't understand that."[8]

Now it was Moore's turn to be angry. When General Schwarzkopf lifted his hand from the briefing chart, General Moore snatched the chart away and quickly began moving down the listed items—bing, bing, bing. His voice was shrill; his large face reddened from the strain. Everyone was on edge. Moore went through the entire briefing without further interruption. When he was finished, there was a long pause.

"I want you to fix this," said Schwarzkopf, in a firm, controlled voice, looking directly at Moore. "And I want it fixed now!" With one hand, the general gathered up the charts that Moore had spread in front of him and said again, "I want you to fix this, and I want it fixed *now!*" Schwarzkopf's gaze shifted to General Horner, who up to this point had said nothing. "Chuck, you go with him."[9]

General Horner stood up and made his way to the conference room door. General Moore collected his charts and papers from General Schwarzkopf, moving quickly to join General Horner. As they walked through the door and out of earshot, Horner said to Moore, "He changed the guidance on you, didn't he?"

Moore nodded, "Yes, sir, for about the fourth time."

"Yeah."[10]

Moore looked at him, anticipating an explanation, but General Horner said nothing else. They walked in silence to the JOC, where General Moore entered the combination code and opened the door for Horner.

The place was just as noisy and hectic as it had been when Horner first visited earlier in the day. Moore led them to a small planning room off the main floor and closed the door. He motioned for his deputy, an Army colonel, to join them. Within minutes, the room was filled with planners, all of whom took turns showing General Horner exactly how they derived the numbers and types of aircraft (both land- and carrier-based) that they used to build the briefing for General Schwarzkopf.

Horner worked with this group late into the night, adjusting numbers, load-outs, and other peripheral aspects of Moore's original plan. They finally agreed on a 15-squadron force structure to slow down an Iraqi advance into Saudi Arabia—if one should come. Horner's intent was to establish a day/night level of effort that would attack primarily the resupply—as opposed to the lead elements—of an Iraqi ground offensive into Saudi Arabia.[11] After the last Vu-Graph was made, copies of the plan were faxed to CENTAF at around 0300 the next day.[12] Shortly after, Horner climbed on board a waiting C-21 along with General Schwarzkopf and the rest of his party for the flight to Washington, D.C.

Sat/4 Aug 90/Wash DC

The Lear jet made its approach into Andrews AFB just before dawn. Washington was already awake. Large numbers of cars and trucks, their headlights probing the early morning darkness, flowed across the bridges connecting Virginia with the District and Maryland. Schwarzkopf, Horner, and the others—fatigued from the previous day's frantic efforts—slowly stirred to consciousness as the sleek, white jet touched down and taxied directly to a parking space in the VIP area.

An entirely too cheerful protocol officer greeted Schwarzkopf's party with a smart salute as they disembarked and ushered them into waiting government vehicles for the trip across town to the visiting officers' quarters (VOQ) at Fort Myer, Virginia. The plan was for everyone to catch a few hours' sleep before meeting with the president. It didn't turn out that way.

General Horner had barely lain down when the phone rang and he was told to meet General Schwarzkopf outside for the short car ride from Fort Myer to the Pentagon. After arriving, they were escorted to the helo pad at the south entrance, where an Army Black Hawk helicopter, its rotors turning, waited to take them to Camp David, the president's retreat. General Powell and SECDEF Cheney arrived soon after and climbed on board.

As the door banged shut, the Black Hawk clattered into the early morning sky and headed north over the Potomac River. It skimmed over the Lincoln Memorial, banked left, and continued in an easy climb over Rock Creek Park. The

9

National Cathedral—a glorious 70-year creation of sweat and stone—slid by on the port side, and then the rolling hills of Maryland came into view. Not many minutes later, the chopper touched down at Camp David.

The secretary's party shuttled from the landing area to the main house in golf carts. The air was cool and pleasant, with just a hint of a breeze—so different from Washington! Manicured lawns and giant, leafy shade trees were everywhere. It was quiet and peaceful. At the main house, they disembarked and went into a large conference room. Most of the president's Cabinet were already there. Secretary Cheney and General Schwarzkopf took seats at the main table. Horner sat behind them. The president was the last to enter.

William Webster, director of the Central Intelligence Agency (CIA), began the meeting with a rundown of events in Kuwait. Schwarzkopf seemed agitated by what Webster was saying and after only a few moments broke into the director's monologue. The general contradicted Webster's assessment of the Kuwaiti situation, saying that he had been in phone contact with a CENTCOM intelligence officer who had been monitoring events from the roof of the US Embassy in Kuwait as the invasion took place. Schwarzkopf's speaking out of turn raised some eyebrows, but what he said generated a round of discussion.[13]

At Cabinet meetings, protocol dictated that only the president's principal advisors were allowed the privilege of open discussion. "Outsiders" invited to the meetings were expected to speak only when asked by a principal or the president himself. Clearly, General Schwarzkopf had stepped out of line, but he was making no apologies. He knew what was happening in Kuwait, and he was anxious for the president to know as well. The picture he painted was one of chaos and sporadic fighting. It was obvious to Schwarzkopf that Iraqi forces had gained the upper hand quickly, having all but destroyed any organized Kuwaiti resistance. The invading Iraqis were firmly in control.

Later in the meeting when Schwarzkopf was *asked* to speak, he stood up and laid out for the president a single-corps ground operation, using the XVIII Airborne Corps and a smaller contingent of marines. He proposed a defensive delaying action, with no amphibious assaults or airborne operations.[14] Schwarzkopf then introduced General Horner, who briefed the plan he had put together with General Moore and the rest of the J-3 and J-4 (logistics) folks at CENTCOM the night before: air power would concentrate on attacking Iraqi resupply lines in order to slow an Iraqi advance into Saudi Arabia.

From the Vu-Graphs Horner used, the president and the Cabinet could tell where the various aircraft would bed down in-theater and what alternative bases they could use if they were overrun. General Horner made it clear that if they attempted to throw everything at the lead elements of an Iraqi invasion, the Iraqis would simply run the CENTCOM forces out of airplanes. In his mind, the best thing to do was to fight a ground war of maneuver and use air power to cut Iraqi sustainment.[15]

During this entire briefing, with its many frank exchanges among Cabinet members, the president said nothing. Only at the end did he ask a number of questions that showed his concern for loss of life and casualties—on both sides.[16] A topic that received some attention from the president was the possible use of Iraqi Scuds.* Horner volunteered that he had spoken earlier with Lt Gen John Yeosock, Third Army commander, about using Patriot missile batteries in an antiballistic missile (ABM) mode to destroy any incoming Scuds that escaped destruction on the ground by allied fighters and bombers.[17] That seemed to end the issue, and the president went on to other concerns.

Over and over, the president kept asking people at the meeting what the principals of the affected countries thought about what was happening. Secretary of State James Baker and Chairman Powell responded by talking about what Prince Bandar, Saudi ambassador to the United States, thought about the circumstances. Bush was not satisfied. He wanted to know what the *principals*, not their representatives, thought about the issues. Surprisingly, the president turned away from

---

*Scuds are surface-to-surface missiles of Soviet origin and are purported to have chemical as well as conventional warheads. Two versions were used in the Gulf War, one of which was developed in Iraq. The Iraqi version has greater range than the standard Soviet missile but a much smaller warhead (approximately 150 pounds versus 500 pounds).

Secretary Baker and gave the task of finding out what Middle East leaders really thought about recent events to his secretary of defense, Dick Cheney. "Dick, I want you to go talk to King Fahd. I will call him this morning. Find out what he thinks about all this."[18]

By 1300 everyone but the president's closest advisors was excused from the meeting. Visitors not familiar with Camp David were given a golf cart "windshield tour" of the facility while they waited for their transport home. Horner and Schwarzkopf were among them. Not many hours later, the two generals were on their way back to MacDill and the enormous problems that awaited them there.

Sat/4 Aug 90/MacDill AFB FL

Dead tired and out of crew rest, General Horner checked into the MacDill VOQ for a few hours' sleep before he flew his F-16 back to Shaw. Thoughts of the last 48 hours flashed through his mind and made sleeping difficult. Just as he was dozing off, the phone rang. It was his own headquarters at Shaw.

"Sir, General Schwarzkopf needs to talk to you on a secure phone."

Horner didn't have a secure phone in his room, so he put on his flight suit and walked around behind the Officers' Club and made his way to General Schwarzkopf's front door. He knocked, and moments later Schwarzkopf came to the door.

"JESUS! How did you get here?" asked the general, somewhat startled. Schwarzkopf was under the impression that Horner had returned to Shaw and had no idea that he was still on base. "Can you go to Saudi Arabia tomorrow?"

"Sure," said Horner nonchalantly, nodding his head as though the general had just asked him to go on a small fishing trip and not fly halfway around the world, leaving his command just when it needed him most.

"Meet me at Andrews at 0900."

"Yes, sir."[19]

That was it. Horner walked back to the VOQ, climbed into bed, and slept soundly the rest of the night. He got up early the next morning, flew back to Shaw, and told his wife he needed enough clothes for two days. She packed a bag for him while he called Bill Rider, his logistician, and asked him if he would like to take a quick trip to Jedda, Saudi Arabia. That done, both men headed out on a C-21 for Andrews in time to rendezvous with Schwarzkopf in Washington at the appointed hour.

0900/Sun/5 Aug 90/Pentagon/Wash DC

For a while, it seemed that no one was going to go to Saudi Arabia because of great confusion over whose airplane— Schwarzkopf's or Cheney's—would be used and who would be on it. Horner sat outside Cheney's office with General Yeosock late Sunday morning while Powell, Cheney, and Schwarzkopf conferred inside. They came out, having decided to go on Cheney's bird, and left immediately for Andrews. Not long after, they were airborne and on their way to the Persian Gulf.

As the brightly painted and polished VC-135 climbed out and headed east over Chesapeake Bay and beyond, an old, battered Pontiac sedan pulled into the deserted parking lot at the Pentagon's south side. From it emerged a slim, sharp-featured colonel. Burdened with books and papers, he awkwardly locked and closed the door of the car with his elbow and hurried down the long walk as fast as his legs could carry him, soon disappearing inside the flat, gray, five-sided building. No one could have guessed that his entry into the planning process would change the course of the impending war and leave generals, secretaries, and even a president in his wake.

Notes

1. Maj Gen Burton R. Moore, USAF, Retired, Tuscaloosa, Ala., transcript of interview with Lt Col Suzanne B. Gehri, Lt Col Edward C. Mann, and author, 21 September 1992, 25, Desert Story Collection, US Air Force Historical Research Agency, Maxwell AFB, Ala. General Moore accompanied General Schwarzkopf to Washington, D.C., and was present at the meeting of 31 July 1990.

2. H. Norman Schwarzkopf with Peter Petre, *General H. Norman Schwarzkopf, the Autobiography: It Doesn't Take a Hero* (New York: Bantam Books, 1992), 294–95.

3. Lt Gen Charles A. May, Jr., USAF, Retired, Washington, D.C., transcript of interview with author, 21 August 1992, 2, Desert Story Collection, US Air Force Historical Research Agency, Maxwell AFB, Ala.

4. Lt Gen Charles A. Horner, Shaw AFB, S.C., transcript of interview with Lt Col Suzanne B. Gehri and author, 2 December 1991, 8, Desert Story Collection, US Air Force Historical Research Agency, Maxwell AFB, Ala.

5. Moore, 21 September 1992, 33.

6. Ibid.

7. Horner, 2 December 1991, 9.

8. Moore, 21 September 1992, 38–39.

9. Ibid.

10. Ibid.

11. Horner, 2 December 1991, 10.

12. The document is in the custody of Dr Diane Putney, a historian with the Center for Air Force History (CAFH), Bolling AFB, Washington, D.C.

13. Horner, 2 December 1991, 11–12.

14. Ibid., 12.

15. Ibid., 13.

16. Ibid., 15.

17. Ibid.

18. Ibid., 16.

19. Ibid., 16–17.

Chapter 2

0905/Sun/5 Aug 90/Pentagon/Wash DC

Once inside the building, Col John A. Warden III, Air Force deputy director for war-fighting concepts, made his way up the wide, south-side corridor, passed the second-floor cafeteria, and took the stairs two at a time to get to his office on the fourth floor. It had been over 48 hours since he had heard the news about the Iraqi invasion of Kuwait, but—up till now—there was nothing he could do about it.

Warden had been vacationing with his wife on a cruise ship in the Caribbean, somewhere south of Cuba, when word of the invasion was broadcast on the Ocean News Network.[1] He had been forced to wait another 36 hours for the boat to steam into Miami before he could get off and head back to Washington. During that time, drinking coffee and gazing into the heavy green seas that rocked the ship as it slowly plowed toward home, Warden became convinced that the Iraqi action would require a US military response. From his years on Pentagon planning staffs, the colonel was afraid that whatever US response was offered, it wouldn't be the right one.

Then and there, he made up his mind to put together a proposal for an effective way to fight the war and to construct a strategy to sell that proposal to the people in the civilian and military chain of command above him.[2] Warden was convinced that the war plans currently in existence were focused almost exclusively on deployment, with only an occasional mention of "defending" an area to which forces were deployed. Warden believed there was no real concept of operations for offensive action in any of the war plans because Americans never conceptualized the world quite that way.[3] He was determined to change that.

Warden's deputy, Col Mike Kiraly, was on leave, so Warden hastily dialed the next officer in line—Col Mike Dunn. As Warden sat in his office, Dunn "backfilled" him on what had happened. Apparently, on Friday the Joint Staff had informally asked the Air Staff for some "suggestions," but despite the Air

15

Staff inputs (most of which came from Warden's directorate), it appeared that the JCS response was going to be a typical cold-war, limited-option sort of thing, with no one really taking the stick and laying out legitimate courses of action for the national command authorities (NCA). At least that's how Dunn and the people in War-Fighting Concepts saw it.[4]

Warden spent the rest of Sunday mulling over what Colonel Dunn had told him and sketching out a plan that would bring together the best minds he could find to work the problem. To begin with, he would use the Checkmate* people and their office space in the basement of the Pentagon as the center of his planning effort. Fortunately for Warden, Air Staff plans to do away with the Checkmate Division had been put on hold almost a year ago, when Warden managed to convince Gen Mike Dugan—then the director of Air Force plans and operations—to put the organization under his direction as a kind of Air Force think tank. It worked well. The officers assigned there—mostly fighter pilots with a sprinkling of tanker, recce, lift, and other support guys, as well as analysts—were able to look at a wide range of plans and contingencies and come up with alternative solutions. Before Warden got hold of this group, they mostly looked at Soviet/US confrontation possibilities. Now they looked at everything.

Mon/6 Aug 90/Pentagon/Wash DC

John Warden assembled his "tiger team" (i.e., his best people) in Checkmate's ramshackle and sprawling offices, not 30 feet from the landmark "purple water fountain."** There were about 25 officers and enlisted people at the meeting, including all of the Checkmate staff and a few folks Warden

---

*Checkmate is a unique directorate in Air Force Plans, whose original cadre included people like Col Moody Suter, famed fighter pilot/interrogator and friend of Soviet MiG-25 defector Lt Victor Belenko. The organization is known for encouraging independent thinking and analysis on important combat-employment issues.

**This is an actual water fountain in the basement of the Pentagon. In the early 1970s, the Air Force officially designated it a "navigation aid." For years, people used the fountain to find their way through the labyrinth of the Pentagon underworld, where rooms appear without reason and stairs often lead nowhere.

had brought in from the Strategy Division and Doctrine Division, as well as other places in the building.

As they stood around in groups of four and five, Colonel Warden outlined his overall strategy on a dilapidated chalkboard. He looked more like a college chemistry professor than a warrior, as he filled the board with circles and hastily drawn lines, stopping only occasionally to answer a question or change a word. In essence, Colonel Warden told the group that he wanted to put together an air campaign based on the five-ring approach he had developed two years ago. (After the Gulf War, this strategy came to be known as "inside-out warfare."[5])

Warden's basic premise was that the modern nation-state consists of five concentric rings—or centers of gravity—the innermost being leadership, then key production, infrastructure, population, and—finally—fielded military forces. Prior to the ascendancy of air power, Warden reminded the group as he wrote on the board, the only way to subdue a nation-state was first to engage and then destroy the opponent's fielded military forces. Until that was accomplished, the other centers of gravity (i.e., other areas also vital to the survival, continued functioning, and will of the nation-state) would be impossible to reach. With air power, he argued, this was no longer the case. All aspects of a nation-state were equally vulnerable to attack and destruction by air power, from the very onset of hostilities.

In Warden's mind, leadership was the real key to success or failure in war. He explained that when an enemy's leaders decided they had had enough, they sued for peace—or someone took power away from them. Therefore, Warden argued, every action in war should be geared to affecting the enemy's leadership, directly or indirectly.

He faced the group and fastened a shirtsleeve button that had come loose during one of his wilder movements at the chalkboard. The fluorescent lights suddenly made him look pale, despite his recent time on the cruise ship. Several strands of hair were sticking up at odd angles, much like the tousled mane of a boy who has just gotten out of bed. He rubbed his hands over his face and continued his monologue.

Leadership, once the most protected and invulnerable aspect of a nation-state, is now a lucrative and extremely vulnerable target. On the other hand, civilian populations—the unfortunate and often powerless victims of hostilities between nation-states—can be left relatively unscathed with the use of modern air power. If for humanitarian or other reasons a combatant nation chose to bypass the population of a hostile nation-state and concentrate on different centers of gravity, this was entirely possible. At least it was in John Warden's mind.

When he finished with his discussions and drawings, the chalkboard was completely full. Centers of gravity had been tentatively identified, and a small number of target categories suggested by the different groups listening to Warden's pitch were already appearing under each of them. Perhaps most curious was the fact that during this entire "discussion," Colonel Warden didn't order anyone in particular to *do* anything. He told the group at large that they needed to get busy and "flesh out" these ideas as quickly as possible. He went on to say that he was looking for small groups of people that could react quickly to changing events—teams that could produce at the lowest level and do things with little standardization.[6]

This came as no shock to the people around him. They were used to the way he did business and his fondness for the "chaos theory"* approach to life and work. Besides, people around Warden understood quite well the premises behind inside-out warfare. They had worked and debated scenarios throughout the past year that highlighted the efficacy of this viewpoint and were eager to apply it to the situation in Southwest Asia. They got to work and, with little fanfare or argument, divided the tasks among themselves.

Before Warden called the meeting in the Checkmate offices that morning, he had discussed his proposal with his boss, Maj Gen Robert M. ("Minter") Alexander, a quiet, thoughtful,

---

*Warden often referred to Tom Peters's book *Thriving on Chaos: Handbook for a Management Revolution* (New York: Alfred A. Knopf, 1987), which argues that a small-staff approach to complex work issues produces high-quality, timely products under "real-world" conditions.

and unassuming man who had spent much of his career in Strategic Air Command (SAC) and was now director of plans. Warden was very candid with Alexander.

"I don't have any idea how it's going to come out, but we are going to put it together anyway and see what happens."

"Fine," said the general.[7]

At that point, neither man realized how all-consuming this task Colonel Warden had taken upon himself would become for everyone involved—in less than 48 hours. Nor did they know whether or not it would gain the credibility it needed to survive the "warlord" world of Goldwater-Nichols.* For the time being, however, General Alexander was content to let Warden pursue the issue as his work load and interest allowed.

Tue/7 Aug 90/Pentagon Basement (Checkmate Area)

At 1000 the next morning, Warden's tiger team met to discuss what they had come up with. Colonel Kiraly—a portly looking, dark-haired fighter pilot—chaired the meeting, while Ben Harvey, a lieutenant colonel, took detailed notes.[8] Lt Col Dale Autry, a Checkmate guy, spoke first. He advocated putting together a briefing based on Warden's inside-out warfare theory. A matrix could be built, using the five rings as starting points. First, they would look at isolating the leadership and Saddam Hussein himself from Iraq. Attrition would have to be factored in, based on desired results. Did they want to destroy or simply control the leadership's means of communicating with its people and its military?

A lively debate ensued between the group members at this point. What became very clear early on was the fact that different risks resulted in different costs, all of which were in some significant way driven by desired results. Next, they looked at what could be done with Iraq's industrial base. They asked themselves many questions: What does Iraq run on?

---

*Under the Goldwater-Nichols Department of Defense Reorganization Act, each CINC has an area of responsibility (AOR) and, with it, the authority to determine how best to plan and execute operations in his theater.

Oil? Electricity? Water? How could those things be taken out? What with? At what cost? From there, the discussion turned to logistics, focusing on the men, machines, and supplies called for in current operational plans to handle contingencies like this one. They were surprised by what they found.

The off-the-shelf plan called for ground forces to be deployed to Saudi Arabia without any real capability to defend themselves from attack. In addition, the kinds of aircraft that would eventually be sent to the theater under the plan were not well suited for a war that could erupt at any moment. The plan assumed a long warning time and large call-up of Reserve forces before they would be forced to fight. That didn't seem very likely to the group meeting in the Checkmate offices this morning.

By 1430 that afternoon, Kiraly's bunch had come to a number of conclusions and were busy putting together slides for a briefing they would give to Colonel Warden in a few hours. In it, they outlined their objections to the current plan and stressed the need to get "serious air power" into the theater as soon as possible.[9] They were looking for aircraft that could be decisive, in order to buy time until a larger contingent of US ground, sea, and air forces could be deployed to the area.

The group also stressed that the existing JCS time-phased force and deployment lists (TPFDL) called for a flow of forces into theater that was, in their estimation, entirely out of line in view of the high possibility of an attack by Iraq.* Lastly, they stressed the need to work up this alternative campaign plan in such a way that it would fit easily within the framework of Joint Staff operations. By so doing, they hoped to ensure that "purple suiters"** could pick it up and run with it.

Not long after, Colonel Warden took the briefing, read a point paper the group had prepared, and outlined essentially everything they had gone over during the afternoon. He made a few comments and changes, offering advice and

---

*Interestingly enough, the Checkmate group's early assessment that there was a high probability of an imminent attack from Iraq into Saudi Arabia changed after a few days and ended up putting the revised Checkmate assessment at odds with Ninth Air Force's. Harvey, 7. (Secret) Information extracted is unclassified (see note 6).

**Army, Navy, Marine, or Air Force people assigned to the Joint Staff are purple suiters. In theory, these people no longer have the parochial view of their service compatriots; hence, they are purple—not Army green, Navy blue, or Air Force blue.

encouragement where appropriate, and returned to his office. When he got there, Lt Col Dave Deptula—a member of the Secretary of the Air Force's Staff Group and a longtime confidant—was waiting to see him. He looked troubled.

Warden had spoken briefly with Deptula early that morning, urging him to find time to come down and work with the group he had assembled in Checkmate. Deptula said he would try to get away, but the work load that Secretary Donald B. Rice was generating simply wouldn't allow it for the time being. Now, here he was. Deptula got right to the point. He told Warden that after talking to him on the phone that morning, he got a call from Col Steve ("Foose") Wilson, head of the "Fighter Mafia" in the Pentagon. Wilson asked Deptula to meet him right away in one of the corridors that ran between their offices. Foose had something to tell him, and it couldn't wait.

After a brief delay to take another phone call, Deptula slipped out of his office and hurried through a maze of drab-colored passageways, past rows of anonymous green doors, before he reached the agreed-upon meeting place. Here, in this seldom-traveled and poorly lit inner corridor, the two men talked. Wilson gave Deptula the disturbing news. JCS had generated a deployment order, and right now, all over the country, aircraft—many, the wrong type of aircraft—were being readied for action in the Gulf. Wilson urged Deptula to go down to the Air Force Command Center, located in the basement of the Pentagon, to see for himself. If he agreed with Wilson that the right stuff was not being sent, he should tell Secretary Rice and get him "energized" on the problem.

Deptula continued with his recounting of the day's events. He explained to Warden that by 1000 he had gotten permission to see the plan and was granted access to the command center. Capt Jim Eckberg went over the deployment with him. It didn't look good. The plan was flowing lots of stuff to theater, apparently with little regard for munitions types and availability. Platforms that could deliver precision guided munitions (PGM) were in short supply. Warden nodded and urged Deptula to continue talking. Everything he was saying seemed to fit nicely with what the folks in Checkmate had concluded in their initial investigation into the deployment scheme.

As they talked, it became obvious that Deptula's concerns were mirrored in John Warden's view of transpiring events. That came as no real surprise to Warden. After all, both men were committed to the same endgame. Deptula had fallen under Warden's influence a year or so earlier when he had worked for him in the Air Force Doctrine Division at the Pentagon. Together, they had explored the high and low ground of aerospace doctrine and war-fighting strategy. Deptula, an F-15 pilot and Fighter Weapons School graduate, was a fast learner and quickly rose to the top of Warden's inner circle. At 6'2" and 215 pounds, Deptula was a big, teddy-bear kind of a guy, who—despite his friendly manner— gave no quarter. Like most people close to Warden, he was never satisfied with a "because-I-say-it-is" type of answer. Unlike Warden, however, he made few enemies and managed to keep himself in the good graces of superiors and subordinates alike. This was to prove invaluable in the coming days.

When Deptula finished, Warden urged him to do whatever it took to free himself from his duties in Rice's office and get down to Checkmate and help build a campaign plan that would work. Warden admitted he hadn't the foggiest idea how he was going to convince the civilian and military leaders it was prudent to do so, but he was determined to try.

0802/Wed/8 Aug 90/Pentagon

The sun made a halfhearted attempt to appear through the hazy morning overcast that filled the Tidal Basin. Although only a few minutes past eight, the air was already warm and heavy. Latecomers, angry and frustrated at having been caught in the snarled Washington traffic, hurriedly made their way toward the many entrances that lined the Pentagon. The lucky ones who had arrived earlier were already at their desks, drinking coffee from seldom-washed cups and spreading the day's work before them. On the fourth-floor "E" ring,* things

---

*Each of the Pentagon's five floors has five corridors—A (innermost) through E (outermost).

were different. There, the smell of freshly brewed coffee wafted through halls of polished marble and mahogany. Secretaries with stiff, coiffured hair, bright summer dresses, and painted nails poured the dark liquid into gold-rimmed cups and answered phones with practiced authority.

One such lady in room 4E936 paused slightly before activating the intercom that connected her with Gen John M. ("Mike") Loh, vice-chief of staff of the Air Force. Someone from General Schwarzkopf's office was on the phone she had just answered. The friendly but official-sounding voice at the other end of the line told her that Gen H. Norman Schwarzkopf, commander in chief of United States Central Command, wanted to speak with whoever was in charge. And he wanted to do it—now.

The secretary was well aware that General Dugan, the Air Force chief of staff, was not in his office, nor even in the building. He was on temporary duty (TDY) to Hanscom AFB, Massachusetts, giving a speech to the Air Force Sergeants' Association.[10] By default, the job fell to the next man in line—General Loh. She buzzed him and told him who was calling. He picked up the phone immediately.

After a brief exchange of pleasantries, General Schwarzkopf, who had just returned from a whirlwind trip to the Middle East, explained why he had called. "You know, I've sent Horner over, and I have got to ask you if I can keep him indefinitely. Will you let me do that because I have got to stay here to get all this other stuff working with Colin Powell, so I'm going to leave him over there if I can." There was a short pause, as if Schwarzkopf wanted to let all that he had said sink in, and then the general added, "He doesn't even have a change of underwear."

"Well," said Loh, laughing at the thought of Horner without a change of underwear and no time to buy any, "he is used to that."

Schwarzkopf chuckled too. "Yeah, he can live in the same underwear for a few months."

Loh became serious. "Look, you *own* Horner! He's yours! I will confirm this with Bob Russ. But you consider that you own Horner." There was an awkward pause while Loh waited for Schwarzkopf to terminate the conversation. They were both four-star generals, but Schwarzkopf was by far the more senior of the two. Besides, he was the one who had called.

"You know," said Schwarzkopf, starting out slowly, almost as though he were thinking out loud, "we have a decent plan for air/land operations, but I'm thinking of an air campaign, and I don't have any expertise—anybody here who can think in those kinds of terms and look at a broader set of targets or a strategic campaign."[11]

Loh could hardly believe what he was hearing! Here was the commander in chief of USCENTCOM—Gen H. Norman Schwarzkopf, an Army infantry officer—hinting around at asking the Air Force for help in building a strategic campaign. General Loh immediately recalled something that Minter Alexander had told him about John Warden's effort in Checkmate. The match was perfect. As a matter of fact, it was almost too [expletive deleted] good to be true! But he had to play it.

"Well," said Loh, running a hand through his thick, black hair and stretching his legs to their fullest, "wait, because we have a cell here that is capable of doing that—that has started talking about that. I will get the support of both TAC and SAC* in helping to flesh that out, and we will start working on that right away and coordinate it with your staff."

Schwarzkopf seized on Loh's offer of coordinated assistance and stressed the need to put something together quickly—something that would work decisively. "I need it fast because he may launch a chemical Scud or chemical attack. We can't go out in piecemeal with an air/land battle plan. I have got to hit him at his heart! I need it kind of fast because I may have to attack those kinds of targets deep, that have value to him as a leader, if he decides to launch a plan of attack with Scuds or with even chemical or nuclear weapons. So, I need this kind of fast."

"Okay," said Loh, already beginning to formulate a plan to give Schwarzkopf exactly what he wanted—and more. "You are welcome to jack it into first gear right now! Okay? I will get

---

*Tactical Air Command existed prior to Air Combat Command (ACC) and was composed primarily of fighter aircraft. Strategic Air Command consisted primarily of bombers, tankers, and intercontinental ballistic missiles (ICBM). Bomber and tanker assets were merged with TAC assets to form ACC in 1992.

back with you. What I need to do is to get a plan going and bring it to you. Give me about a week."

Schwarzkopf responded immediately, "I'm going to call Colin Powell now and tell him that we have talked and that you are working this for me."

"Fine," said Loh, thinking to himself as he put down the receiver and flicked a piece of dust off his shirtsleeve, "I've got to go talk to Colin Powell now and make sure that we are all working together."[12]

General Loh reached across his desk and hit a button on his squawk box that connected him directly with General Alexander. "Minter, get your fanny up here!"[13] While Loh waited for his chief planner, he placed a call to the TAC boss, Gen Robert D. Russ. As soon as Russ came on the line, General Loh began to tell him about his call from General Schwarzkopf.

"He probably should have called you, but he called me," said Loh apologetically. "He wants to know if Horner can kind of be given—if he owns Horner for the indefinite future. I said, 'Of course you do!'"

"Sure he does," growled Russ. "I have essentially told his staff that."

"Okay, fine," said Loh, relieved that Russ at least agreed with him as to the disposition of Horner. "Also," he went on cautiously, "Schwarzkopf needs some planning help because he wants to look at a set of targets beyond the traditional tactical targets that we have been planning against for CENTCOM. He wants to look at the broader set of strategic targets. I'm going to talk to Chain, and I've already got the Checkmate guys looking at this."[14]

Loh was careful not to put too much emphasis on the Checkmate involvement in the planning process. He knew that Russ, as commander of TAC, might resent or misconstrue what was being done on his or CENTCOM's behalf in Washington. After all, Horner, as Ninth Air Force commander, belonged to Russ—not Loh or any other four-star general in the Pentagon, for that matter.

It was tacitly understood by the "brotherhood" of fighter-pilot generals that Bob Russ was the senior active duty member of that elite group. The fact was, at one time or another, General Russ had been the boss of all these men—including the current chief, General Dugan—so no one wanted to make him mad unnecessarily.[15]

"Okay," said Russ, somewhat confused by exactly what General Loh was asking him for.[16] "Our guys are pretty good at this. We have already got a cell that I use with CINCLANT* with the B-52s that are chopped** to CINCLANT that talk about long-range missions. Let me get our planners that have worked this before, because we have already been in this with CINCLANT, and they can pitch in and help."[17]

The conversation ended pleasantly enough a moment or so later. For his part, unbeknownst to Loh, General Russ put no stock at all in Loh's insistence that General Schwarzkopf himself had asked for help in identifying and planning "strategic targets." On more than one occasion, Russ had seen people, especially staffers, invoke the name of key figures to achieve their own objectives. As far as he was concerned, this could have been just another example of this kind of posturing. In any case, he would get Brig Gen Tom Griffith, his deputy chief of staff for plans, to work on this right away and tell him to make sure that Chuck Horner knew what these guys in Washington were up to.

Shortly after getting called on the squawk box by the vice-chief, General Alexander spent a frantic few minutes trying to locate Colonel Warden. He found him down in the Checkmate offices, working on the plan. Alexander told Warden to meet him in General Loh's office immediately. They arrived in the vice-chief's office within minutes of each other and ended up cooling their heels in the outer lobby while Loh talked on the phone with Russ. Bits and pieces of Loh's conversation spilled through the open door and were overheard by Warden and Alexander. Until then, neither man had been certain as to why Loh had summoned them. Was it good news or bad? Now they had a pretty good idea. Loh caught Alexander's eye and motioned both men into his office. The vice-chief then carefully explained the gist of his

---

*Commander in chief, United States Atlantic Command.

**From "change of operational procedures" (CHOP). The gaining unit has tactical control but not command of the assets.

conversation with General Schwarzkopf and ended by reiterating his understanding of what the commander of CENTCOM wanted: "He wants a strategic air campaign."[18] Loh then shifted in his seat, looked directly at both men, and dropped the bombshell concerning when he had promised to deliver this whole thing to Schwarzkopf—and whom he expected to produce it.

"Put together and brief a strategic air campaign for me, and let me see what you have." Both Warden and Alexander struggled with the realization of what they were being asked to do and the ridiculously short time frame they had to accomplish it in. Warden spoke first.

"Well," he said, trying hard to contain the thoughts and emotions that stirred inside him at this crucial moment, "we are working on one; we will have the first cut sometime this afternoon for you to take a look at."[19]

Once again, Loh made it clear that he was eager to see the briefing as soon as it was ready. He thanked both men for coming and then dismissed them.

Right after they left, General Loh had his secretary put in a call to Gen John ("Jack") Chain, SAC commander. It went much smoother than his earlier call to Russ and didn't take nearly as much time.

"Good," said General Chain after hearing of Schwarzkopf's request for Air Force help in building a strategic plan and of Loh's decision to have Alexander and Warden head up the effort in the Air Staff to put one together. "I will talk to the plans guys, and I will provide whatever support you need."[20]

General Loh hung up the phone, very pleased with the morning's events. He made a note to brief General Dugan as soon as possible and looked forward to seeing what Warden and Alexander could come up with. It wouldn't take long.

Warden could barely contain his excitement as he walked back toward the plans area with his boss, General Alexander. Talk about luck and good fortune! Only days before, he had been agonizing over how he could contact and then, hopefully, convince the senior leadership of the necessity for a hard-hitting air campaign against Iraq, and now he is told by a person no less than the vice-chief himself to put one together! Even more incredibly, he is told that Gen H. Norman

Schwarzkopf—the commander of USCENTCOM—is the guy who first asked for such a plan and was now waiting for it to be delivered by the Air Staff!

Warden's mind raced with all sorts of ideas: who to call, how to tell the folks already assembled in Checkmate, what kind of time line they should use, what approach to take, and so forth. Even though General Loh had spoken of the need to make it a "joint" plan, Warden had other ideas—at least for now. He thought to himself, "Okay, but I can't do that right off because what I'm going to do is to use Air Force resources to lay out the thing initially." In the back of his mind, he had already decided that the whole effort might be possible using Air Force assets alone. As far as he was concerned, that would be a good thing—a very good thing.[21]

When he reached his office, Warden immediately picked up the phone and started calling people he had contacted earlier to work on the project. It was only a handful of people, really—most were from other divisions within the Air Staff, and of course there was Colonel Deptula from Secretary Rice's office. He asked them to drop whatever they were doing and meet him in the Checkmate area at 1000. At the appointed hour, a group of about 30 people gathered to hear what Warden had to say.

He began by telling them about his meeting with General Loh and the mandate he and General Alexander had received less than two hours before to produce a strategic air campaign. Warden hammered home what an extraordinarily important thing it was that this group was undertaking. Over and over, he emphasized that this air campaign planning effort they were committing to was not some silly paper exercise but a deadly serious attempt to match national objectives with military power. Real lives would be at stake, he told them. It would be hard work. No one knew how it would come out or whether or not it would be accepted. Because of these incredibly high stakes, Warden urged the group to give everything they had to this effort; nothing less than their individual and collective best efforts would suffice.[22]

Warden pointed to the rings on the chalkboard and the rapidly growing target sets people had written alongside. "This is what we are going to call the plan; it's going to be Instant Thunder." Warden chose the name as a direct contrast to the ill-fated, Vietnam-era plan entitled Rolling Thunder, which called for slow and gradual escalation of air activities to allow the enemy time to rethink his predicament and, hopefully, sue for peace. "This is not your Rolling Thunder. This is real war, and one of the things we want to emphasize right from the beginning is that this is not Vietnam! This is doing it right! This is using air power!"[23]

He clasped his hands and looked out over the group of people in that paint-peeled, overcrowded room. They all were confident and ready to go. Warden was more determined than ever to avoid the air power mistakes of the past: too little, too long, and too late. Instant Thunder would see to that. Within minutes of his announcement, the name and concept were accepted by the rest of the group assembled in Checkmate that morning, and by noon all the Vu-Graphs bore that title.

The last portion of the meeting included a brief discussion of the short-term game plan, Checkmate area organization, and division responsibilities. People quickly broke off into ad hoc working groups, most of which had been established over the past two days and had gotten started. It didn't take long to consolidate the previous day's planning efforts into a workable briefing format. By 1245 Warden's group was in General Alexander's office going over the Vu-Graphs they would use with General Loh. One of the leadoff transparencies listed four presidential "objectives."* This was a bit of sleight of hand on Warden's part. The listed presidential objectives were, in fact, pieced together by the folks in Checkmate from recent speeches and statements made by President Bush. No one questioned them, so this Vu-Graph was quickly followed by another showing corresponding military objectives.** Alexander, with little fanfare or adjustment, approved what

---

*Early versions of Instant Thunder showed four presidential objectives:
"1. Iraqi withdrawal from Kuwait.
2. Restore Kuwaiti sovereignty.
3. Secure free flow of oil.
4. Protect U.S. lives."
**Military objectives shown in early versions of Instant Thunder were
"1. Force Iraqi withdrawal from Kuwait.
2. Degrade Iraq's offensive capability.
3. Secure oil facilities.
4. Render Hussein ineffective as an Arab leader."

was presented and accompanied Warden and the rest of the Checkmate party to their 1300 meeting with General May.

As the assistant deputy chief of staff for Air Force plans and operations, May was still sitting in for Jimmie Adams, who was away on vacation. He was somewhat uncomfortable with General Adams being out of town and with the pace of events occurring around him. Both May and Adams were wary of Warden and his uncanny ability to push whatever program or policy he deemed important around and—often—over them. Too many times before, Adams or May had told Warden to forget about something he had gotten excited about, only to see it come back as a direct tasker from the chief or a civilian authority.[24]

It was no secret that General Dugan, Air Force chief of staff, thought highly of Warden. When Warden's book, *The Air Campaign: Planning for Combat,*[25] was released by National Defense University Press in the fall of 1988, Dugan—then a three-star—ordered that a copy be given to every officer on the Air Staff.* Dugan himself wrote the cover letter that accompanied the distribution of Warden's book.

All of these things weighed on General May as he took the briefing from the small group Warden had assembled in his office. As a straight-shooting, company kind of guy with a lot of years in the bomber (B-52) community, May was at a loss to understand what motivated Warden to put himself so far out on a limb so many times with his bosses and others, on issue after issue. As far as May was concerned, it was presumptuous and arrogant of Warden to continue to push things that his immediate superiors thought better of. Still, May had to admit that on many occasions, Warden was on the right track. As far as he could tell, Warden never did anything for personal gain or glory. To the contrary, Warden's actions made him many more enemies than friends.

General May deferred a direct critique of the presentation and instead insisted that arrangements be made to give General Adams a full update on everything they had done as

---

*At the time, General Dugan was Air Force deputy chief of staff for plans and operations and had created a special position for Colonel Warden in the Plans Directorate.

soon as Adams returned to the Pentagon. This requirement had no effect on the plan's immediate status. Truth was, with the briefing due in General Loh's office in only a few minutes, the planning train was "leaving the station," and May was going to ride it whether he liked it or not.[26] General May reluctantly gave his tacit approval and joined the group as it made its way down the fourth-floor E ring to the vice-chief's office.

General Loh's reaction to the briefing was far better than anyone expected. He embraced the way Warden and his people framed the problem with their concept of a five-ring nation-state and directed that they expand their effort to identify target sets, strategies, weapons requirements, and airlift, and then incorporate all of this into not only a cogent briefing but an executable strategic air campaign plan for General Schwarzkopf's approval—by Friday.

"This is the number one project in the Air Force," said Loh, with obvious enthusiasm. "You can call anybody, anyplace that you need, for anything."[27] No one had spoken sweeter words to Warden in his entire life! He left the meeting determined to take the general up on his promise.

Warden wasn't the only one intent on making use of Loh's "anybody, anyplace, anything" chit. General Alexander put in a call to Maj Gen James R. Clapper, Jr., the head of Air Force intelligence.

"I need some help," began General Alexander. "I need some of your best intel guys. General Loh wants us to put a strategic air campaign together."

Clapper did not respond immediately. When he finally did, his tone was guarded. "Why are you doing this?"

"Jim, I haven't got time to discuss it," said Alexander, somewhat perturbed and a little surprised at Clapper's reaction to his request. "General Loh has asked us to do this."[28]

Clapper came back as slowly as before, his voice strained and more than a little on edge. "This is Horner's job."[29]

"Yes," said Alexander grudgingly, as he glanced up at the model of the B-2 bomber that sat prominently on his desk. It was becoming obvious that, for whatever reason, Clapper was not interested in playing. Neither man said anything for a few seconds, and then Clapper spoke up.

"I was down at Ninth just before they deployed. They *have* a strategic air campaign. They already have one."

For a while, General Alexander thought Clapper had really stumbled onto something. Had Schwarzkopf called Loh without really being aware of the fact that Horner and the folks at Ninth Air Force had a handle on this all along? That notion was quickly dispelled, however. After Alexander asked him what the campaign consisted of, Clapper explained, "They have about 44 targets."

In truth, Clapper had no idea what Alexander was even talking about! In the intelligence general's mind, targets and target folders equated to an air campaign. Most of the targets he had seen at Ninth were interdiction and counterair targets. In no way, shape, or form could any of this be construed as a bona fide air campaign. Alexander tried to explain this to Clapper but to no avail. Despite Alexander's best efforts, he could not persuade General Clapper to give any of his people to the effort now going on at the Air Staff. Although Clapper was polite, he made it clear that no help would be forthcoming.[30]

Frustrated, General Alexander immediately called General Loh.

"General Loh," said Alexander, trying hard to suppress his pique with General Clapper, "Jim Clapper says that General Horner already has a strategic air campaign and that this is not necessary."

Loh's response was immediate and to the point. "Schwarzkopf wants it! You put it together, and you tell Clapper to get some people down there to help you!"[31]

Alexander called Clapper back. It seemed to take a long time for the general to come to the phone. When he finally got there, Alexander told him what Loh had said. Despite this new edict from Loh, Clapper still sounded unwilling to support the Air Staff effort. He was convinced that Ninth Air Force had a strategic air campaign plan and that Loh, Alexander, and the rest of the boys were getting into Horner's mess kit. He wanted no part of it.[32]

Wed/8 Aug 90/Bolling AFB/Wash DC

The message that Alexander had relayed from Loh must have had some effect on General Clapper because later the same day, Clapper called Col Jim Blackburn, his director of targets, and told him to send somebody to the Checkmate area to "find out what they were up to there."[33] Blackburn had been contacted earlier in the week by Colonel Warden and was familiar with what the people in Checkmate were trying to accomplish. Like his boss, Colonel Blackburn was suspicious of the Air Staff operation.

In Blackburn's mind, ad hoc groups like Warden's had a way of taking on a life all their own, sucking up organizations and talent, and in the process destroying carefully laid out, formal networks—especially those that connected intelligence organizations with their operational customers in the field. He said as much to Warden earlier in the week when Warden spoke of getting as much information as he could from as many sources as possible.[34] Operators—taking direct inputs from the CIA, DIA, the National Security Agency (NSA), and others—would, in Blackburn's opinion, produce lots of half-baked conclusions without the benefit of skilled intelligence fusion.

Reluctantly, Blackburn detailed one of his majors to head over to Checkmate and report back later in the day on what he had discovered. Blackburn called Warden and told him he was sending a targeteer over per General Clapper's instructions and asked that he be given clearance into the Checkmate facility. Warden readily agreed to do so.

Wed/8 Aug 90/Pentagon (Late Afternoon)

General Alexander touched base with Warden and several of his people throughout the hectic afternoon. Except for the run-in with Clapper, things were going quite well, considering. It occurred to him that the best thing to do might be to simply call Ninth Air Force and invite their staff to come up and assist on the planning effort. After all, they were the ones who would have to live with it. He put in a call to Shaw AFB. What he found there wasn't very encouraging.

Horner was already deployed to the Gulf with a large contingent of his best people. The ones left behind were trying hard to cope with the situation but were overwhelmed by calls coming in from everywhere asking about aircraft schedules, loadouts, munitions requirements, beddown locations, and a myriad of other questions related to the CENTAF deployment.[35]

To make matters worse, communications with Horner and the rest of the CENTAF people in-theater were almost nonexistent at this time.* Tenth Air Force, a Reserve outfit, was supposed to backfill the departing Ninth Air Force people, but it simply wasn't happening. Their response to General Alexander's request was predictable: "Well, we'll see. If we haven't got anybody, we can't make them available."[36]

Alexander hung up with the dawning realization that not everyone was going to jump on this air campaign bandwagon. Maybe there were a lot more people out there like Clapper and the guy he just talked to. Maybe the idea of a strategic air campaign was not as firmly embedded in the hearts and minds of Air Force people as he had always believed. Maybe. He and the rest of the growing Checkmate crowd would soon find out.

Thu/9 Aug 90/Pentagon

By 0740 General Alexander, Warden, and a few of the other planning-team members were in the vice-chief's office, explaining the previous afternoon's events and the progress they had made on the plan.[37] Alexander brought up his conversation with Ninth Air Force, telling Loh that as far as he could tell, Ninth—or even TAC for that matter—wasn't going to send anyone to help. Loh was sympathetic and nodded his

---

*Things were so chaotic at Shaw during this period that within several days, General Russ, TAC commander—on the recommendation of his assistant director of operations and without consultation with the Ninth Air Force commander, General Horner—ordered all remaining Ninth Air Force personnel to deploy to the command post at Langley AFB, Virginia, and declared Langley as "CENTAF Rear." In a TAC-generated message given wide dissemination per General Russ's orders, Maj Gen Mike Ryan, TAC director of operations, was named "acting commander" of CENTAF Rear and took charge of all deployment-related tasks for CENTAF. Headquarters TAC personnel then augmented the Ninth Air Force people and formed the bulk of the CENTAF Rear contingent. This arrangement remained in effect throughout the buildup, war, and postwar period. Russ, 9 December 1991, 41–43 (see note 15).

head in understanding. He picked up the Instant Thunder briefing package and put it in front of Alexander. "Okay, fax this thing down to TAC and get their comments."[38] Loh made it very clear that he was confident that all the big guys—Schwarzkopf, Chain, Russ, Dugan, and even Colin Powell—were behind this effort. He wanted it to proceed at "full speed."[39]

A short discussion followed, concerning how to identify the key targets critical to the survival of Saddam Hussein and his infrastructure. Ben Harvey, who up to now had been frantically trying to write down what had been said, volunteered that it might be useful to get the inputs of academics like Prof Ed Luttwak* and others. Loh agreed but cautioned that he didn't want any of them read in on the plan. They would simply talk to them and get their ideas on the situation.[40]

It was matter-of-factly announced that the Instant Thunder briefing would go to General Schwarzkopf on the afternoon of the tenth and to Chairman Powell early the next morning—on Saturday. The meeting lasted only a few minutes longer, and by 0800 Warden and the others were headed back down to the basement where they welcomed the SAC augmentees who had arrived in response to General Loh's call to the SAC commander.[41]

Most of the SAC guys were pilots or navigators, very familiar with the workings, capabilities, and requirements of the bomber and tanker fleets. After a short briefing on what the planning effort consisted of so far and after a review of the tasking, these crew members were assimilated into the ad hoc Checkmate organization as "system specialists"** and immediately put to work.

---

*Dr Luttwak holds the Arleigh Burke Chair in Strategy at the Center for Strategic and International Studies, Washington, D.C. Since the early 1970s, he has served as a consultant on strategic matters and has conducted military studies on a variety of topics, including the first rapid-deployment force concept (the basis of CENTCOM).

**As system specialists, the SAC people were assigned to "Campaign Plans and Applications Organizations," which was cobbled together by Colonel Deptula and approved by Colonel Warden. It served to give form and shape to the evolving planning effort. Campaign Plans and Applications Organizations Chart, 11 August 1990, Deptula files 03–3A, Desert Story Collection, US Air Force Historical Research Agency, Maxwell AFB, Ala.

Things happened quickly throughout the rest of the morning. By 0900 Checkmate had a copy of the 44 CENTAF targets General Clapper had spoken to Alexander about the day before. The people in Checkmate overlaid these targets on top of their own and began work on aiming points and other critical data on the entire set. Arrangements were made to meet with Professor Luttwak later in the afternoon. Other scholars would follow.*

Long before lunchtime, General Alexander ordered the Instant Thunder briefing sent not only to TAC, as Loh had requested, but to SAC and Air University (AU) at Maxwell AFB, Alabama, as well. Warden was opposed to sending the plan anywhere at this stage. He argued that it would be better to get it all worked out, present it to General Schwarzkopf tomorrow, and then send it wherever Alexander thought it should go.[42] Alexander wouldn't buy it. He wanted to be up-front with all the war fighters and anyone else who might ultimately be involved in the planning. He wanted to start building a constituency—to make people feel they were participants in the process. The briefing was faxed out as ordered.

Notes

1. Col John A. Warden III, Washington, D.C., transcript of interview with Lt Col Suzanne B. Gehri, 22 October 1991, 36, Desert Story Collection, US Air Force Historical Research Agency, Maxwell AFB, Ala.
2. Ibid., 36–37.
3. Ibid., 10.
4. Ibid., 39.
5. Ibid., 39–42.
6. Notes, Lt Col Ben Harvey, 2, Desert Story Collection, US Air Force Historical Research Agency, Maxwell AFB, Ala. (Secret) Information extracted here and in subsequent references is unclassified. Hereinafter referred to as Harvey.
7. Warden, 22 October 1991, 40.
8. Harvey, 5.
9. Ibid., 6.

---

*Ultimately, Warden and Alexander met with Luttwak, Colin Gray, and Eliot Cohen, as well as a host of people from the Rand Corporation. None of them were at all familiar with the effects and capabilities of PGMs, and they spoke mostly in generalities. Alexander, 30 May 1991, 9–11 (see note 19).

10. Gen Michael J. Dugan, Washington, D.C., transcript of interview with author, 15 August 1991, 3, Desert Story Collection, US Air Force Historical Research Agency, Maxwell AFB, Ala.

11. Gen John M. Loh, Langley AFB, Va., transcript of interview with Lt Col Suzanne B. Gehri and author, 19 September 1991, 4–5, Desert Story Collection, US Air Force Historical Research Agency, Maxwell AFB, Ala. It is important to note that this dialogue is General Loh's recollection of the conversation—not General Schwarzkopf's. Despite repeated requests, General Schwarzkopf did not grant the author an interview.

12. Ibid., 6.

13. Gen John M. Loh, Langley AFB, Va., transcript of interview with Lt Col Suzanne B. Gehri and author, 26 September 1991, 7, Desert Story Collection, US Air Force Historical Research Agency, Maxwell AFB, Ala.

14. Ibid., 9.

15. Gen Robert D. Russ, Alexandria, Va., transcript of interview with Lt Col Suzanne B. Gehri, Lt Col Edward C. Mann, and author, 9 December 1991, 36–37, Desert Story Collection, US Air Force Historical Research Agency, Maxwell AFB, Ala. In his interview of 26 September 1991, Loh commented that part of the reason he didn't say much about the Checkmate involvement to General Russ was that "he [Russ] might have said, 'Okay, we will take over this. Don't you do anything.' After all, he outranked me" (page 10).

16. Russ, 9 December 1991, 9.

17. Loh, 26 September 1991, 9.

18. Warden, 22 October 1991, 49.

19. Lt Gen Robert M. Alexander, Washington, D.C., transcript of interview with Lt Col Suzanne B. Gehri, Lt Col Edward C. Mann, and author, 30 May 1991, 2, Desert Story Collection, US Air Force Historical Research Agency, Maxwell AFB, Ala. See also Warden, 22 October 1991, 49.

20. Loh, 26 September 1991, 13.

21. Warden, 22 October 1991, 49.

22. Ibid., 50.

23. Ibid., 52–53.

24. Gen Jimmie V. Adams, Eglin AFB, Fla., transcript of interview with Lt Col Suzanne B. Gehri and author, 3 February 1992, 22, 41, Desert Story Collection, US Air Force Historical Research Agency, Maxwell AFB, Ala.

25. John A. Warden III, *The Air Campaign: Planning for Combat* (Washington, D.C.: National Defense University Press, 1988).

26. Harvey, 8.

27. Warden, 22 October 1991, 51.

28. Alexander, 30 May 1991, 6.

29. Ibid.

30. Ibid.

31. Ibid., 7.

32. Ibid., 8.

33. Col James Blackburn, Bolling AFB, Washington, D.C., transcript of interview with Lt Col Suzanne B. Gehri, Col Edward C. Mann, and author, 21 April 1993, 13–20, Desert Story Collection, US Air Force Historical Research Agency, Maxwell AFB, Ala.

34. Ibid.
35. Alexander, 30 May 1991, 9.
36. Ibid.
37. Harvey, 10.
38. Alexander, 30 May 1991, 9.
39. Harvey, 10.
40. Ibid.
41. Ibid.
42. Warden, 22 October 1991, 54.

Chapter 3

Thu/9 Aug 90/Langley AFB VA

It had been raining on and off in the Tidewater area since early morning. Thunder, low and rumbling, marshalled in each new wave of fast-moving clouds, pelting the ramps and taxiways at Langley AFB with heavy rain. At times, it was almost impossible to see the ghostly shapes of the 1st Tactical Fighter Wing's Eagle jets arranged in neat rows along the perimeter of the field. Somehow, the high-tech birds looked delicate and fragile as they sat exposed to the blustery elements. Not far away in a headquarters building, Tom Griffith, TAC's director of plans, was wrestling with a few storm problems of his own.

A copy of Instant Thunder had come over the secure fax from General Alexander and the boys in Air Force Plans with a note asking for comments. Griffith put a few of his people together and asked them to take a look at it. Cols Dick Bigelow, Alex Bettinger, Doug Hawkins, and Rich Bristow were huddled on the other side of the base, poring over the document and trying to come up with a reasonable response for General Griffith to take to General Russ before they sent anything to the Pentagon.

The whole operation was very close hold. Just the day before, Russ had called Griffith over to the command section and told him to "start thinking about if we were to do anything over in Saudi Arabia, Iraq, or Kuwait. Develop some options of what force structure we would take over there and what you would do."[1] Now this new twist! Neither Griffith nor his four colonels could understand what the people in the Air Staff were doing mucking around in CENTAF business!

Bettinger and Hawkins were strongly opposed to Instant Thunder from the start, thinking it was "too violent" and not at all in the "best interest of the Air Force."[2] One of their first orders of business was to try to send the plan to General Horner in Riyadh, Saudi Arabia. It wasn't easy. Repeated attempts to send the document into theater via secure—and

39

even unsecure—fax failed. The reason was simple: Horner's communications equipment was not fully functioning at this early stage of the deployment.

Bristow and Bigelow were not as adamant in their criticism as were Bettinger and Hawkins, but they too thought the plan was flawed. Bristow complained that Instant Thunder lacked a "tactical perspective" because it failed to commit forces to holding a defensive line on the Kuwaiti/Saudi border. To him, Warden's plan for selective bombing amounted to nothing more than a new twist on the old Douhet-era practice of indiscriminate bombing.[3] All four officers shared concerns about the plan's apparent lack of integration with ground forces. Where was the Army scheme of maneuver? How will air support it? When will the Army be there? They could find no answers to these questions in Instant Thunder. The men rejected the plan and gave their reasons for doing so to General Griffith.

The general basically concurred with the group's findings. However, instead of thanking the four colonels for their efforts and letting them go back to their normal routines, he asked them to stay together and work on a credible TAC alternative to Instant Thunder—something General Russ (and, more importantly, General Horner) could use. The men retired to a third-floor office in the plans complex and began work on their new tasking.

Meanwhile, Griffith gathered up the Instant Thunder papers scattered across his desk, stuffed them into a manila folder, and headed across the street to see Bob Russ. The rain had abated somewhat, so he managed to get to the headquarters building with only an occasional drop of water falling on his starched, open-collar blue shirt. Even though using an umbrella was "legal," the gruff-looking former Army-helicopter-pilot-turned-Air-Force-general couldn't bring himself to do that. It just didn't seem right. Russ's executive officer—a clean-cut, pencil-thin, fighter-pilot colonel—waved Griffith through the outer office and into Russ's private chambers.

Once inside, Griffith went over Instant Thunder with Russ, page by page. The general, too, had many reservations about what he was seeing and told as much to Griffith. His biggest concern was the fact that Chuck Horner—the commander in-theater, the guy who would have to execute the plan—had no input![4] Russ wanted to make sure that "we didn't have someone picking targets in Washington [sic], like they did in Vietnam, and the poor guy out in the field saying, 'That is the dumbest thing I have ever seen!'"[5]

Griffith concurred, remembering with some dread a phone call he received from General Alexander shortly after the Instant Thunder fax arrived at Langley. Alexander told him, "Hey, we think the national leadership is going to want to start doing this . . . in about two or three weeks."[6] Griffith was convinced that the Instant Thunder air campaign was absolutely the wrong thing to do in light of the fact that no serious ground forces would be available in such a short time. Both Russ and Griffith agreed that "if we drop the first bomb, we had better have enough Army out there to prevent Hussein from driving to Riyadh and picking up General Horner and throwing him in the back of a pickup truck!"[7]

Another vital aspect Russ felt was missing from Instant Thunder was anything on electronic countermeasures (ECM). He was certain the whole ECM arena—from strike-package configuration to suppression of enemy air defenses (SEAD)—needed to be very carefully developed, and he knew that Horner didn't have anyone to do it. Russ's gut feeling was that Brig Gen Larry Henry, a well-known and respected weapons system officer with a rich background in defense suppression tactics and technologies, could handle the job. He made a mental note to tell Mike Ryan, his director of operations, to pass that bit of information on to Horner, first chance he got.[8]

Both men discussed some selective options that made more sense to them than the massive attack called for in Instant Thunder. Russ simply didn't believe that the American public would support an all-out war.[9] Instead, he advocated a demonstration of US power and resolve. One option involved sending F-117s against a nuclear reactor and power plant rebuilt by the Iraqis after the Israelis took it out several years before. His idea was to hit the target and announce to Saddam Hussein, "Look, we have the strength to take out *anything* in your country at *any* time and at *any* place that we want to, as demonstrated by what we did here."[10] Such an action could be a unilateral, one-time option or a precursor to other things.

Griffith leaned forward as Russ warmed to the idea and carried it a little further. If such an action were taken, he mused, the president could let Saddam think about it for, say, 12 hours, and then if nothing happens, go back the next night and take out two more of his storage and production facilities. Let him think about *that* for a while, and if nothing happens, go back the next night and take out *three* sites. If no response, then "go for the gusto!"[11]

Russ felt that these actions would show the tremendous capability of the United States and would demonstrate to Saddam Hussein that "with air power, we had the ability to operate anywhere in his country, at any time, and destroy whatever we wanted."[12] Russ told Griffith to run with these ideas and get back to him as soon as he could with something on paper. The one-star agreed to do his best, stuffed the Instant Thunder fax back into its folder, and left.

Later that same day, Griffith met again with his colonels to hear what they had come up with. Their concept, pitched in the general's spartan and poorly appointed office, called for a massive air strike on Iraqi forces *in Kuwait*, as well as the use of air-to-ground fighters to help defend the Saudi border if the Iraqis started to move south.[13] They even added a "little bit of a ground campaign [to] win the war."[14] Griffith asked a few questions and then hurried across the street to show the new plan to General Russ.

It wasn't long before a downcast Griffith shuffled back to his office and threw the manila folder containing the TAC alternative on his desk. In the room were the four colonels and a few of the plans and intelligence folks who had been rolled into the TAC planning effort. Griffith told them General Russ had not accepted the plan as written, saying it needed more work. He talked to the group about General Russ's idea of a demonstration plan involving the targeting of nuclear, biological, and chemical (NBC) facilities and the rapid (two-to-three-day) escalation of hostilities if Hussein didn't withdraw his forces from Kuwait. Some of the officers who heard Griffith were visibly upset, arguing that "this is a throwback to the Vietnam era."[15] Griffith was unmoved. They worked on into the night and all the following day, trying to put together something that Russ would approve.

Fri/10 Aug 90/Langley AFB VA

By early evening, Griffith's planners were confident they had something the boss could live with. Russ had left his office hours ago, but Griffith arranged to take his party to a meeting at the commander's private residence later that night.

In the meantime, Colonel Bettinger's secretary, Zunelle ("Z") Bookhardt, had managed to type all of Instant Thunder—and an alternative TAC plan—into an encoded message format and send it over the wire to General Horner at US Military Training Mission (USMTM) in Riyadh.[16] Horner quickly read the message, frowned, and scribbled in the margin, "Do with this what you will. How can a person in an ivory tower far from the front, not knowing what needs to be done (guidance), write such a message? Wonders never cease."[17] He tossed it into his out basket and went on to other things.

Griffith drove slowly past the Langley Officers' Club, wishing he had time to stop and get something to eat before he saw Russ. Instead, he turned down a small side street marked "for residents only" and made his way to the TAC commander's house. It was readily visible, even in the darkness. General Russ had the biggest, most impressive house on base. Built in the 1930s, when air power was still in its infancy, the rambling, two-story, brick-and-stone house looked out over a shallow, saltwater bay populated by a wide variety of ducks and other waterfowl. In summer and on early autumn days, a stream of colorful sail and powerboats paraded past the house on their way to and from the Atlantic Ocean. Nearby, but far less imposing, were similar houses of key members of the TAC staff. All of the residences had been built as public works projects during the Great Depression to house high-ranking Air Corps officers. Now they were home to a new generation of Air Force generals charged with the care and feeding of a large and powerful fighter and attack force.

Griffith pulled up in front and walked around the car to the sidewalk. The carefully manicured lawn glistened under the old-fashioned streetlamps. It was quiet and peaceful. The only sound was the hushed footsteps of the four colonels, who had driven their own cars, as they fell in trail behind Griffith and made their way to the front door. Griffith rang the doorbell,

43

and he and his party soon were ushered inside. Mrs Russ was in the kitchen preparing the evening meal. The general motioned the group into his study, a small room filled almost to overflowing with books and memorabilia. Once everyone was inside, he softly closed the door, turned to them, and said, "Well, when they ask you what you did for the war, you can tell them you were over here, you sat in my study, and we worked out the plan."[18]

The men listened while General Griffith gave Russ a rundown on the reworked plan. It incorporated Russ's earlier concerns and showed US forces initially attacking a single nuclear facility and then pausing six to 12 hours to give the Hussein regime an opportunity to respond. If the Iraqis did not respond favorably, our forces would conduct larger and more powerful strikes against targets in both Iraq and Kuwait. Russ's total approval of this escalation plan was somewhat surprising to Griffith.[19] He had expected the general to play with the wording or edit out entire portions of the text, but Russ made no changes.[20] It wasn't at all like him.

After the briefing, Russ sat back in his chair and ruminated aloud his views on how the crisis should be handled. This new TAC plan provided just exactly what was needed—a demonstration of firm US resolve to eject the Iraqis from Kuwait. Unlike the Instant Thunder crowd, he didn't want to go in there with guns blazing. Privately, he thought that Warden's bunch was "a group of hair-on-fire majors in Washington that [thought they] were going to win the war all by themselves."[21] Russ had been in the joint arena too long to believe that anybody would ever allow the Air Force to operate alone.[22]

Colonel Bristow had been fidgeting on the edge of the couch ever since Russ started talking. He broke in, "Sir, you know this looks a whole lot like Vietnam—this idea of demonstration and then standing back and seeing what is going to happen."[23] General Russ looked at Bristow and smiled, "Rich, the problem is, in today's era, the people and the political situation are not right for an all-out war."[24] In Russ's view, the American press and public would simply not support it. Besides, the kind of intense activity called for in Instant Thunder was downright dangerous! If not properly controlled,

44

the fighting could spread to other areas in the Middle East and beyond. Bob Russ did not want any part of a plan that, in his view, could put the United States in the position of starting World War III. That was something he simply couldn't tolerate.[25]

Russ ordered Griffith's team to take the TAC plan to Washington as soon as possible and work with the folks in the Pentagon. He explained again to Bristow and the others that the outcome he was looking for was a tactically sound plan that would have the support of the American people and would result in the Iraqis leaving Kuwait.[26] There was little discussion after that. Griffith and the rest of the group stood, bid the general and his wife—who had been graciously holding supper all the while—a good night, and left the house.

Once outside, Griffith and the colonels lingered under the streetlamp near their parked cars, discussing the evening's events. Alex Bettinger made it clear he didn't want to go to Washington. He was already working with Maj Gen Mike Ryan and the other TAC planners, trying to make some sense of the logistics flow into theater. He was simply too busy with beddown problems to head off to D.C. and wrestle with John Warden and his group. Besides, the other guys were more than up to the task. Griffith listened patiently, nodding his head in agreement. Since none of the others seemed to mind, the general decided that Bristow, Bigelow, and Hawkins would leave for the Pentagon the following morning.[27]

Before they could go, however, Griffith wanted the entire TAC plan—the one Russ had just approved—faxed up to General Alexander's office to give those Pentagon guys something to think about. Little could he know that the fate of Instant Thunder and the entire air campaign had, for the most part, already been decided.

Notes

1. Brig Gen Tom Griffith and Col Alex Bettinger, Langley AFB, Va., transcript of interview with Lt Col Suzanne B. Gehri and author, 26 September 1991, 7, Desert Story Collection, US Air Force Historical Research Agency, Maxwell AFB, Ala.
2. Ibid., 2.

3. Col Richard D. Bristow, Langley AFB, Va., transcript of interview with Lt Col Edward C. Mann and author, 9 November 1992, 4, Desert Story Collection, US Air Force Historical Research Agency, Maxwell AFB, Ala.

4. Gen Robert D. Russ, Alexandria, Va., transcript of interview with Lt Col Suzanne B. Gehri, Lt Col Edward C. Mann, and author, 9 December 1991, 19, Desert Story Collection, US Air Force Historical Research Agency, Maxwell AFB, Ala.

5. Ibid., 19–21.

6. Griffith/Bettinger, 26 September 1991, 11.

7. Ibid., 15.

8. Russ, 9 December 1991, 21.

9. Bristow, 9 November 1992, 10.

10. Russ, 9 December 1991, 11.

11. Griffith/Bettinger, 26 September 1991, 10–11.

12. Russ, 9 December 1991, 13.

13. Bristow, 9 November 1992, 5–6. Colonel Bettinger destroyed all copies of this plan, and none are now known to exist.

14. Ibid., 5.

15. Ibid., 6.

16. Griffith/Bettinger, 26 September 1991, 19.

17. Message, 100145Z Aug 90, Tactical Air Combat Operations, Langley AFB, Va., to commander, CENTAF, deployed, chief, USMTM, Riyadh, Saudi Arabia. (Secret) General Horner's handwritten comments on the document are unclassified.

18. Bristow, 9 November 1992, 9.

19. Giffith/Bettinger, 26 September 1991, 19.

20. Ibid.

21. Russ, 9 December 1991, 23.

22. Ibid.

23. Bristow, 9 November 1992, 11.

24. Ibid.

25. Ibid., 10.

26. Ibid.

27. Griffith/Bettinger, 26 September 1991, 4.

Chapter 4

Thu/9 Aug 90/Pentagon/Wash DC

Standing in front of General May's expansive, paper-strewn desk, General Alexander could hardly believe what he was hearing! The speaker phone was on, and May was talking with Mike Ryan, TAC's director of operations, about the Instant Thunder plan that Alexander had faxed to Langley earlier in the day. "I like everything after the last slide,"[1] said Ryan, his voice distorted and tinny as it came through the gray speaker box that sat half-buried under a pile of May's paperwork. The acerbic comment cut like a knife through Alexander, and his round, bespectacled face twisted in pain. May noticed and gave him a wry "I told you so" kind of grimace, as he listened to the TAC general go on about why he thought Instant Thunder was so far off the mark.

Alexander hardly heard the rest of the conversation. The quiet, soft-spoken general could not fathom why anyone, let alone TAC, would have such a visceral reaction to the Instant Thunder planning effort. It wasn't as though he or any of his people were grandstanding! General Schwarzkopf himself had asked for assistance, and they, in good faith, had been working the problem as diligently as possible! Why this horrible fuss over the Air Staff's attempt to deliver a workable plan to an operational CINC? Was it a matter of mucking with somebody else's rice bowl? Was that what TAC's dislike for Instant Thunder really boiled down to? He didn't know—at least not yet.

May's reaction to Ryan's critique, however, was very different from Alexander's. He had never been too keen on either the plan or Warden's shenanigans. His boss, Lt Gen Jimmie Adams, felt the same way. Despite the fact that Adams was on vacation, May had called him several times that week to keep him updated on the directorate's activities. Adams indicated that he was concerned about the Air Staff getting involved in this kind of war planning. It could send the wrong signals to a lot of people. In May's mind, General Ryan's comments confirmed that Instant Thunder had already done that—at least in the eyes of TAC's leadership.

Later, as Alexander slowly walked back to his office, oblivious to the faster-paced younger officers and enlisted people who swirled past him in the corridors, it occurred to him that General Ryan and probably all of TAC thought he and Warden were out of their minds! How could there be such controversy over something as straightforward as strategic attack? How? He was absolutely floored![2] Back at his desk, Alexander picked up the secure phone and called Lt Gen Charles G. Boyd, commander of Air University. Alexander had been talking with Boyd about Instant Thunder, on and off, for the past several days, and the AU commander had been very encouraging. Maybe he could offer some suggestions on what to do next.

The call went through, and Alexander quickly filled Boyd in on the TAC response. Registering no surprise, the general reminded Alexander that he had warned him it wouldn't be easy to convince people of the soundness of the Instant Thunder plan. A lot of folks, including a sizable contingent of Air Force people, were suspicious of any view that made air power anything more than an adjunct to ground operations. In General Boyd's view, this permanent subordination of air power to ground attack was crippling and dysfunctional. Tens of thousands of US ground troops might lose their lives if air power were squandered away piecemeal instead of being employed as Air Force doctrine intended it to be. Boyd had said as much to Alexander in earlier conversations. Warden too.

The conversation ended minutes later with Boyd promising Alexander a quick response on the Instant Thunder plan from a small group of Air University people who, per Boyd's instructions, had been poring over the document since it arrived on the classified fax machine.* Boyd told Alexander that, as far as he was concerned, the plan was "right on."[3]

---

*The US Air Force Wargaming Center at Maxwell AFB, Ala., faxed AU's comments to General Alexander at 1930, 9 August 1990. Surprisingly, they were very critical of Instant Thunder and even took exception to the plan's strategic objectives, saying they were "inappropriate and probably counterproductive." The entire critique bore an uncanny resemblance to the one prepared by General Griffith's people at TAC, which advocated a demonstration of the capability to destroy targets of "high national value." Fax from USAF Wargaming Center to Director of Plans, Headquarters USAF, Deptula file 5, Desert Story Collection, US Air Force Historical Research Agency, Maxwell AFB, Ala.

Alexander carefully placed the phone back in its cradle and gazed out his fourth-floor window at the airliners climbing out over the Potomac from National Airport. He watched for a long time, undisturbed and totally immersed in his thoughts about the internal Air Force conflict over the application of air power. As he thought, the exact meaning of what Boyd and Warden had been talking about slowly dawned on him.[4]

Alexander and Warden made several more trips to General Loh's office that morning for a final "tweaking" of the Instant Thunder presentation they were scheduled to give to General Schwarzkopf the next day. They shifted a few targets, including some communications nodes, from one category to another and removed the slide on strategic rings after TAC insisted it was an "academic bunch of crap."[5] All and all, though, the thrust and content of the original briefing remained unchanged.

In the late afternoon, General Ryan called back to Washington and made it clear that his boss, Gen Bob Russ, was not happy with the Instant Thunder plan. He cautioned General May that it was imperative the Instant Thunder briefing team not speak to Schwarzkopf before they personally came down and briefed the TAC folks, including General Russ. Taking Ryan's warning to heart, May quickly called in General Alexander and ordered him "not [to] brief Schwarzkopf without briefing TAC."[6] Alexander was in a real fix now because the flight had already been set up for a direct trip from Washington to MacDill AFB in Tampa. The only person with the authority to change that was Gen Mike Loh himself, and it was getting very late in the staffing process to do that.

Fri/10 Aug 90/Pentagon/Wash DC

Minutes before the morning staff meeting, Alexander and May pulled General Loh aside and spoke with him about the briefing schedule. Alexander was uncharacteristically direct: "General Adams said we must go down there, and TAC says we must come down there and brief them first." May nodded his agreement. Alexander hesitated for an instant, as though thinking better of it, but then blurted out, "General Russ wants to see this!"

Loh said, "Well, okay."[7]

In the blink of an eye, the whole issue had been decided. To all appearances, the briefing schedule was set in stone—first TAC, then CENTCOM. Warden, however, couldn't live with the arrangement. Shortly after the morning staff meeting with General Loh broke up and most of the participants had left, he took the general aside and proposed that instead of going to TAC, they take the briefing to Hanscom AFB in Massachusetts for General Dugan's personal review. Warden argued that this approach would eliminate any squabbling about who had final authority on what was being presented to General Schwarzkopf. General Loh—dark circles forming under his eyes from lack of sleep and the strain of trying to mollify TAC, yet produce a credible option for General Schwarzkopf—shoved his hands deep into his pockets and walked a short distance from Warden, head down, weighing the proposal. Warden stood waiting near the doorway a long time before General Loh finally turned to him and nodded his consent. The general then hurried off to call Dugan to advise him of the change in plans.[8]

Loh reached the Air Force chief of staff on the first try and explained John Warden's idea of bringing the Instant Thunder briefing to Hanscom for his personal review. The chief quickly rejected the suggestion and told Loh to forget about coming up to see him—or stopping at Langley for that matter. Time was of the essence. Dugan made it clear that he was comfortable enough with Warden and the Instant Thunder plan to allow Warden's team to brief it to Schwarzkopf now. He told Loh to send them directly to MacDill.[9] The conversation ended minutes later with Loh agreeing to do as he was told.

Not 15 minutes after Warden's meeting with General Loh, Minter Alexander was about to walk out the door on his way to Andrews AFB, where he would catch a plane that would take him first to Langley and then, if all went well there, to MacDill. His secretary stopped him just as he was walking through the door, waving frantically and pointing to the phone. General Loh was on the line, and he wanted to talk with him now! Alexander put the receiver to his ear and set his slim, leather briefcase down with his free hand. "I've changed my mind," said Loh in a very matter-of-fact tone. "Go straight to see Schwarzkopf. Do not go to TAC."

For a moment, Alexander didn't know what to say. He couldn't believe the vice-chief was going to take on the TAC commander, four-star-general Bob Russ—a man who was senior to Loh by a full six years! Unaware of Loh's earlier conversation with General Dugan, Alexander couldn't make sense of this change of plans, especially after Loh had been told only hours before by both May and Alexander that his own operations and plans deputy, Gen Jimmie Adams, had made it clear that going to TAC was the prudent thing to do! What was going on? he asked himself, as his right hand absentmindedly adjusted the few gray hairs he had left on his balding head.

"Don't call them or anything. You just go straight to see Schwarzkopf."[10]

The call was over almost before it began, yet it changed everything. "Loh is fearless,"[11] thought Alexander as he walked away. He had never seen anybody like him. But then again, he had yet to meet H. Norman Schwarzkopf. He would get his chance soon enough.

At 1030 the small executive jet carrying Alexander, Warden, and three additional planners* lifted off from Andrews AFB and quickly disappeared into the leaden skies. Alexander and Warden wasted no time pulling out their briefing materials and going over the Instant Thunder presentation with the other men, looking for any flaws that might weaken their case or, worse yet, cause them to fail. They discussed at length the slide on the importance of Arab "face" and talked about General Dugan's search for innovative thinkers to handle Arab cultural questions as they related to the conduct of the war.[12]

The team then discussed Gen Lee Butler's reaction to the Instant Thunder briefing that Warden had given him a few hours before they took off for MacDill. A key member of the JCS, Butler was considered by many to be one of the brightest

---

*The planners Warden selected to attend the briefing were Lt Col Ron Stanfill, Lt Col Ben Harvey, and Lt Col Larry Eckberg. Harvey, 15. (Secret) Information extracted is unclassified (see note 8).

and most capable Air Force generals on active duty. Warden and Alexander knew that Butler's support of the Instant Thunder plan would be very beneficial in the joint arena.

Happily for both men, General Butler's reaction to the plan had been favorable. The more he heard about it, the more he liked it, exclaiming, "Excellent, excellent! This is the exact opposite of what we did in Vietnam! This is what we want!"[13] Despite his enthusiasm, Butler stopped short of agreeing to jump in and take full sponsorship of the plan for the Joint Staff.[14] Instead, he asked General Alexander to brief him on Schwarzkopf's assessment of Instant Thunder as soon as they returned. Full support from anyone in the JCS would simply have to wait.

At 1245, as the plane nosed over and began its descent into MacDill, the team members stowed the briefing materials and returned to their seats. Warden mused aloud that if they could get Schwarzkopf's approval no later than the 12th, they could be ready to execute by the 18th! That would allow enough time to implement a deception plan that had coalition forces slowly building to strike Kuwait, when in fact a sizable air armada of the right aircraft could, within days, go after the very heart of Saddam Hussein's power base—Iraq itself.[15]

Palm trees and brightly colored houses tucked neatly into the recesses of Tampa Bay gradually increased from toy- to life-size as the jet carrying Alexander and Warden flared onto the runway at MacDill and taxied to a halt. When the hatch opened, a flood of warm, tropical air entered the cabin, fogging over the windows and making things damp and sticky. Warden tugged at his collar and tried to smooth the wrinkles that rapidly appeared in his uniform as he and the rest of the party clambered into vehicles that took them to the monolithic structure which served as Schwarzkopf's headquarters.

Once inside the building, they were escorted through the security checkpoint and began winding their way through a labyrinth of corridors. Alexander and Warden spotted the familiar face of Burt Moore, the USCENTCOM operations director. They greeted each other warmly, and as they walked along the narrow passageway, Moore explained that the Instant Thunder briefing would take place in his office—not General Schwarzkopf's. Furthermore, only Schwarzkopf,

Moore, and the deputy commander, Gen Buck Rogers, would attend from the CENTCOM side.

The J-3's office was on the first floor of the building, well back and several corridors removed from the main entrance. Once they arrived, Moore ushered the group inside. The nondescript outer office, occupied by a stern-looking secretary, had several wooden desks and an ancient, overstuffed leather couch that rested on a worn-out carpet that should have been replaced ages ago. Even the paintings on the walls looked as though they belonged to a different time and place. The men grew restless as they stood with briefcases and slides in hand, trying to engage in small talk as they waited for generals Rogers and Schwarzkopf to arrive.

It didn't take long. The two senior officers entered, and General Moore quickly introduced them to Alexander and his party. Schwarzkopf was carrying a large omelette and a glass of milk, which he took into Moore's inner office.[16] This room, although smaller than the outer office, was better decorated and more cheerful. A large, neatly arranged walnut desk was at one end of the room, while the other end contained a small conference table and chairs. Schwarzkopf ambled over to the table and seated himself. The others joined him, their backs to a wall covered with flying memorabilia gleaned from Moore's many years as a fighter pilot.

Warden sat on Schwarzkopf's left and gave him the briefing, using paper copies of the Vu-Graphs the team had brought with them. The colonel was very upbeat and didn't appear at all intimidated as he spoke to the CINC. He began by introducing the Instant Thunder plan by name, referring to it as a proposal for a strategic air campaign, and then quickly outlined the reasons such a plan could and should be implemented.

From there he moved into a discussion of objectives—first presidential, then military. Warden made certain that Schwarzkopf was aware of the deliberate links between the military and presidential objectives and their relationship to the campaign in general. He made no mention of the fact that the presidential objectives were nothing more than selected segments of White House news releases and recent presidential speeches that the Checkmate planners had pieced together. Neither Schwarzkopf nor the other two CENTCOM officers questioned him.

The strategy behind these objectives was elegant in its simplicity—destroy Saddam Hussein's ability to wage war by destroying targets critically important to his regime. Doing so, Warden argued, would require pitting US strengths against Iraqi weaknesses—specifically, US air and naval power against Iraqi air defenses. The Iraqi army was big, in place, and very casualty tolerant. Many months would pass before enough US ground forces and equipment could be brought in-theater to challenge Saddam's troops in a confrontation that might be too late and—just as important—too bloody. Instead, Warden advocated selective destruction of key Iraqi targets, most of which were within Iraq itself. Warden laid out target sets within each of the five categories included in his nation-state model (minus the ring chart). Under the leadership category, he talked about incapacitating the Hussein regime by destroying targets such as civil and military telecommunications and C^2 nodes. The key production category included targets such as power storage and distribution stations as well as internal oil distribution and storage terminals. The colonel cautioned against destroying Iraq's oil production capability for fear the nation would not be able to pay any war debts or rebuild itself after hostilities. He paid particular attention to ridding Iraq of its NBC production and research facilities, emphasizing that this target set had to be destroyed if Iraq were to cease being a threat to the rest of the world.[17]

The Iraqi railroads formed a single target set under the infrastructure category. These lucrative targets would be easy to hit in the desert because their locations were well known and hard to hide. The right laydown of munitions would produce huge bottlenecks of enemy supplies, which were excellent targets themselves. In keeping with Instant Thunder's concept of operations, which called for an absolute minimum of civilian casualties and collateral damage,[18] Warden excluded direct attacks in the population category. Instead, he advocated strategic and tactical psychological operations (PSYOPS) that focused on isolating the Hussein regime from the Iraqi people, foreign workers, and conscripted soldiers serving in Kuwait.

Warden paused a moment and looked around the room. Lt Col Ben Harvey, one of the Checkmate planners, had just come through the door after being denied access earlier due to a problem with the transfer of his clearance.[19] He sat down with the two other Checkmate people on the far side of the room and attempted to make himself as inconspicuous as possible. Generals Rogers and Moore had sat impassively as Warden talked and now were simply staring at him, waiting for the other shoe to fall. But Schwarzkopf, who had contented himself at the beginning of the briefing with slowly chewing on his omelette and drinking milk, was now eating much faster and almost smiling. It made for an odd combination—the burly general's mouth slightly open, chewing and grinning at the same time.[20]

Warden pressed on, outlining attacks against Saddam Hussein's strategic air defense system as well as his entire offensive air capability. Under the Instant Thunder plan, the fielded forces (the fifth category) that would be subjected to violent attack and massive destruction would be Hussein's bombers, fighters, missiles, and their control mechanisms (i.e., air defense facilities, radar sites, launch centers, etc.). The ground forces in Kuwait and those in Iraq near or on the border would be attacked only if they attempted to move forward out of their positions and into Saudi Arabia. This restriction would avoid laying waste to Kuwait in an attempt to restore it.

Warden showed how a mix of approximately 500 aircraft could do the whole job in six to nine flying days (i.e., in good weather), but—as he told Schwarzkopf—he would need some changes in the deployment flow to pull it off. If the general gave approval no later than 12 August, A-10s could be moved up to counter any Iraqi armored advance. Further, an increase in the number of B-52s, F-117s, and F-111s would allow the strategic air campaign to start as early as 18 August. Warden stepped through the execution phase of Instant Thunder using a series of charts that succinctly explained why each target set was being attacked, what kinds of things made up the target set, and how the targets would be neutralized.

As Warden briefed the final stages of the plan's execution phase, Schwarzkopf's demeanor made it clear that the general was pleased with what he was hearing. But generals Rogers and Moore were not. In fact, Moore interrupted Warden as he started to talk about striking the palace bunker in Baghdad and other facilities included in the leadership category: "Watch what you are saying! I'm not exactly sure about this."[21]

Before Moore could finish, Schwarzkopf's voice boomed, "That's exactly what I want!" Up to this point the CINC had said nothing, but now he was talking fast, his face animated and full of energy. "Do it!" he said. "You have my approval—100 percent! This is absolutely essential! I will call the chairman today and have him give you a directive to proceed with detailed planning immediately."[22]

The general half stood, leaning forward and resting his massive hands on the small conference table. He looked big in his battle-dress uniform (BDU) and polished boots—bigger and stronger than he did when he came into the room. It was as though someone had just lifted a heavy burden off his shoulders. Many of the things Warden had been talking about had been circulating in Schwarzkopf's mind for days, but he hadn't been able to articulate them. Now, after seeing Instant Thunder, he had a clear idea of what he needed to do.

"I have briefed the president on a lot of elements of this, but lots of folks are leaning backwards, saying it is too hard to do," said Schwarzkopf, looking directly at Moore and Rogers. He turned and faced Warden, almost leaning over him.

"You have restored my confidence in the United States Air Force. CENTAF can't do planning. Do it the way you want," he said, nodding his head.

"It is up to the Air Force. [expletive deleted], I love it!" Schwarzkopf exclaimed loudly, slapping his hand on top of the briefing charts. "You are the first guys that have been leaning forward. I'm glad to see it. This is exactly what I want!"[23]

The CINC picked up the briefing material and held it out in front of him. "We are dealing with a crazy man, and he is going to lash out. We can't afford to have [just] options to fall back on!* He will attack Saudi Arabia, do something nasty to the hostages, drop chemicals on Israel. This is where America has the edge!" Schwarzkopf paced around the table, talking to no

---

*This comment about not being able to rely solely on "options" reveals Schwarzkopf's frustration with the limited military responses advocated by CENTAF and CENTCOM planners at that time.

one in particular. "If we invade Kuwait," he mused, "they will destroy it. This might leave Kuwait intact." He walked over to Moore's desk and turned to the group. "After you do this," he said, holding the Instant Thunder papers up for everyone to see, "we will drop leaflets on his frontline forces and tell them they are out of business. If they don't believe it, let them try and call home! Your [expletive deleted] is next!"[24]

A small discussion on some of the details concerning the plan ensued, but after Schwarzkopf's rousing endorsement, neither Rogers nor Moore offered any serious objections. General Alexander spoke up: "We need to get TAC involved."

But Schwarzkopf simply ignored the comment and continued thinking aloud. "I'll tell the chairman. What do you lose by planning? So what if it leaks? It took us a long time to do this in Vietnam, and we never did it in the Iranian hostage [crisis]!"

Alexander piped in, "We will throw everything at it!"

"I'm with you," said Schwarzkopf, shaking the Instant Thunder papers in front of Alexander. "This will lower losses. We must get this to the chairman before Monday!"[25] Turning to Warden, the general continued, "Okay, now I've got some additional instructions for you. I want you to think about some other options, one of which is using Turkey. Can I use Turkey, and if I use Turkey, put together another option for using Turkey. Tell me how soon I can do this—what we would have to change in order to do it very quickly. Give me some feel on the logistics and so on."[26]

Alexander was uncomfortable during this whole exchange. He knew that his boss, General Adams, would not be happy if the Air Staff ended up shoulders deep in CENTCOM planning, especially if TAC were not given an opportunity to take the lead. He cleared his throat and addressed Schwarzkopf in his calmest voice. "Now, sir," he said, reaching for the Instant Thunder charts, "we are going to have to take this to TAC and let TAC get to work on this."

Schwarzkopf exploded. "No!" he shouted, poking a finger at Alexander, "I want you to do it." He gave Alexander and Warden a week to flesh out the Instant Thunder plan and bring it back to him in an expanded and executable form.[27]

The meeting broke up 30 minutes after it began. Schwarzkopf lingered for a few minutes in the doorway of Moore's office, talking to the lieutenant colonels who had accompanied Warden and Alexander to MacDill. Alexander was still at the table talking with General Moore when he saw Warden walk over to Schwarzkopf, touch him lightly on the shoulder, and tell him that the Instant Thunder plan would make a hero out of him, "[in the same] category [as] MacArthur and Patton." Alexander was horrified! Such an outlandish comment could jeopardize everything they had done to this point and take them out of the planning process altogether. What possessed Warden to say such a thing to a four-star general he didn't even know less than an hour ago? Warden, with his almost passionate belief in air power and his overwhelming confidence in the Instant Thunder plan, had gone too far this time. Unfortunately, Alexander was in no position to save him. To Alexander's amazement, however, Schwarzkopf loved the comment! He smiled broadly, puffed out his chest, and strode confidently from the room.[28]

After General Rogers left, Moore closed the door to his inner office and huddled with Alexander and the other Air Staff planners. He cautioned them that despite Schwarzkopf's enthusiasm and apparent endorsement of the Instant Thunder plan, any changes that they might want to make in the deployment flow would be difficult because of base saturation problems. Furthermore, changes tended to displace a lot of other vital "stuff" that needed to get to the theater. Moore suggested they send one or two people down to his directorate to help coordinate activity on the plan.[29] Alexander agreed to work with Moore on these issues.

Warden and the lieutenant colonels finished putting away the briefing materials while Alexander and Moore continued their conversation. As they packed, Moore's secretary knocked softly on the door, walked into the room, and told them their transportation to the airfield was waiting outside. Moore stood, wished them a speedy trip back to Washington, and excused himself, explaining he had to return to the operations center.

Outside, the air was hotter and even more humid than when they had arrived two hours earlier. Warden scarcely noticed. He was elated with the turn of events and utterly preoccupied with preparing a briefing for General Powell, as well as planning his return visit to Schwarzkopf. His mind raced, trying to figure out how much time he would have before briefing Powell and how best to approach this most influential of four-stars. At the terminal, he got an answer to one of his questions. Alexander announced that Schwarzkopf's office had just advised him the meeting with the chairman was set for 0930 the next morning in General Powell's office. Warden would have to figure out the other answer for himself—in less than 16 hours.

Notes

1. Lt Gen Robert M. Alexander, Washington, D.C., transcript of interview with Lt Col Suzanne B. Gehri, Lt Col Edward C. Mann, and author, 30 May 1991, 10, Desert Story Collection, US Air Force Historical Research Agency, Maxwell AFB, Ala.

2. Ibid., 10, 14.

3. Ibid., 14.

4. Ibid.

5. Ibid., 12.

6. Ibid., 12, 15.

7. Ibid., 15.

8. Notes, Lt Col Ben Harvey, 15, Desert Story Collection, US Air Force Historical Research Agency, Maxwell AFB, Ala. (Secret) Information extracted here and in subsequent references is unclassified. Hereinafter referred to as Harvey.

9. Ibid.

10. Alexander, 30 May 1991, 15, 16.

11. Ibid., 15.

12. Harvey, 16.

13. Alexander, 30 May 1991, 25.

14. Harvey, 16.

15. Ibid.

16. Lt Gen Robert M. Alexander, Washington, D.C., transcript of interview with Lt Col Suzanne B. Gehri, Lt Col Edward C. Mann, and author, 3 June 1992, 16, Desert Story Collection, US Air Force Historical Research Agency, Maxwell AFB, Ala.

17. Col John A. Warden III, "Desert Storm Air Campaign," presentation to the USAF Air and Space Doctrine Symposium, Maxwell AFB, Ala., 6–8 April 1993. A hard copy of Colonel Warden's slides is in the Desert Story Collection, US Air Force Historical Research Agency, Maxwell AFB, Ala.

18. Ibid., 3.

19. Col John A. Warden III, Washington, D.C., transcript of interview with Lt Col Suzanne B. Gehri, 22 October 1991, 63, Desert Story Collection, US Air Force Historical Research Agency, Maxwell AFB, Ala.

20. Alexander, 3 June 1992, 16.

21. Alexander, 30 May 1991, 17.
22. Ibid., 16, 28.
23. Ibid., 17, 28.
24. Ibid., 28–29.
25. Ibid.
26. Warden, 22 October 1991, 64, 66.
27. Alexander, 30 May 1991, 17.
28. Ibid., 16.
29. Harvey, 17.

Col John Warden leads an Instant Thunder planning session in early August 1990 in the Checkmate office at the Pentagon.

Board in the Checkmate office in the Pentagon shows Instant Thunder development and initial taskings laid out by Col John Warden on 8 August 1990.

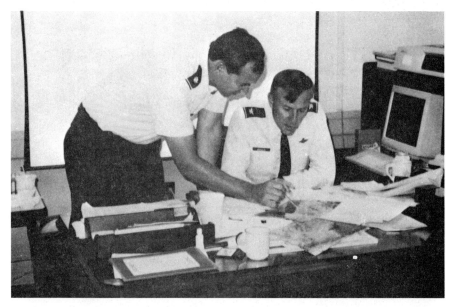

Lt Col Dave Deptula (left) and Col John Warden discuss Instant Thunder planning in August 1990.

Maj Gen Minter Alexander (foreground) receives early version of the Instant Thunder briefing from Col John Warden (second from right) in August 1990.

Lt Col Dave Deptula (center) gives Instant Thunder rundown to TAC "spies" Col Dick Bigelow (left) and Col Rich Bristow (right) on 11 August 1990.

Col John Warden (left) and Lt Col Ben Harvey (center) with Navy captain Gregory Johnson of the CENTCOM staff at MacDill AFB, Florida, after briefing General Schwarzkopf on 17 August 1990.

Lt Col Dave Deptula (kneeling, left), Lt Col Ben Harvey, Lt Col Ron Stanfill, and Col John Warden (standing, left to right, in flight suits) outside the flight operations building at Andrews AFB, Maryland, prior to departure for Riyadh on 18 August 1990.

Col John Warden (note all three F-15 squadron patches on his 36th Tactical Fighter Wing flight suit) at Andrews AFB, Maryland, prior to departure for Riyadh on 18 August 1990.

Lt Col Ben Harvey, Col John Warden, Lt Col Dave Deptula, and Lt Col Ron Stanfill (left to right) go over the Instant Thunder plan one more time on the way to Riyadh on 18 August 1990.

Posted results at day's end (30 January 1991) during the Gulf War.

Col John Warden (front row, center) surrounded by his Checkmate mafia at war's end (March 1991).

Air power statement written by Lt Col Dave Deptula at war's end in the Black Hole planning cell on 28 February 1991.

Chapter 5

Sat/11 Aug 90/Pentagon/Wash DC

John Warden took a deep breath and began briefing Gen Colin Powell, chairman of the Joint Chiefs of Staff (CJCS), on the Instant Thunder plan. Although the chairman shared the large, round conference table with 12 high-ranking officers and civilians, Warden addressed his remarks exclusively to Powell. His voice was controlled and measured, with barely a hint of the pent-up nervous energy and sleeplessness he had felt during the last 16 hours. Some of the JCS big guns were there, including Adm David Jeremiah, vice-chairman; Lt Gen Mike Carns, director of the Joint Staff; Lt Gen Tom Kelly, director of operations; and Lt Gen Lee Butler, director of strategic plans (J-5).

The Air Force team consisted of generals Loh, May, and Alexander, as well as a sprinkling of Checkmate planners who managed to find the cheap seats along the wall. Warden went through the plan in much the same fashion he had with Schwarzkopf the day before. After the colonel finished, Powell pushed his chair back from the table, clasped his hands, and said, "Good plan! Very fine piece of work!"[1]

Alexander, obviously pleased by Powell's reaction, cautiously explained to the chairman and the others at the table that Instant Thunder was not something that could be done piecemeal. This comment came as no surprise to the men who had worked on the plan. Since returning from MacDill, they had discussed possible service reactions to Instant Thunder, one of their biggest concerns being an Army comment along the lines of "You can take out the leadership, but don't hit the bunkers." Consequently, Alexander took great pains to prevent any such mutilation of the concept, explaining to Powell that Instant Thunder was an integrated plan and that chopping it into parts would certainly destroy it. Loh interrupted Alexander with a wave of the hand and pointed to the briefing slides in front of Powell: "It *is* a highly integrated plan like the Bekaa Valley [Lebanon] but more *massive* than Linebacker [Vietnam]."[2]

71

Powell nodded and turned toward Warden, who had been fidgeting nervously while the generals talked. "The strategic air campaign cuts out the guts and heart, but what about the hands?"

Warden drew himself up to his full height and answered confidently, "The strategic air campaign will isolate Hussein, virtually assuring that most forces could walk home."[3]

A short discussion ensued between Warden and the chairman on the diversion of Instant Thunder resources to handle additional taskings. "Now, General," said Warden, his voice growing hard and a little edgy as it became clear that Powell was thinking about diverting some of Instant Thunder's aircraft to ground support, "one of the things we really need to be careful about is that if there's some action on the ground, you can't reroll the strategic air campaign. You've got to press with the strategic air campaign. We made that mistake in World War II, and we don't want to do that again."[4] The retort was pure Warden, and the people in the room who had never seen him in action before were appalled at his audacity and candor with the chairman. General Alexander, all too familiar with Warden's antics, was beginning to turn pale.

When the topic turned to additional centers of gravity, Warden explained that he wanted to hit the Republican Guard in Iraq but was opposed to taking out the ground forces along the front lines in southern Kuwait. The colonel was convinced that if anyone could overthrow Saddam, it was the conscripted army he would leave as cannon fodder to replace his elite Republican Guard invasion force when the latter pulled back from the front. According to Warden, that army might very well march home en masse and defeat what was left of Saddam's loyal forces. That accomplished, a new leadership formed from within the conscript army could establish a new and more favorable government in Iraq.

General Powell listened patiently and when Warden finished, said in a low, even voice, "If we go this far in the air campaign, I want to finish it. Destroy the Iraqi army on the ground." His fingers drummed out a silent rhythm on the highly polished table as he looked into the faces of the men who had brought him the plan. "I don't want them to go home. I want to leave smoking tanks as kilometer posts all the way to

Baghdad."[5] The room became quiet as the enormity of Powell's statement sunk in. Even the air-conditioning fans, which were barely audible before, now seemed loud and abrasive.

General Kelly was the first to speak. He had sat icily through Warden's entire presentation, but the chairman's comments seemed to bring him back to life. "Well," said Kelly, "air power has never worked in the past by itself; [ne-e-e-ver] worked in the past by itself. This isn't going to work. Air power can't be decisive!" Kelly bolstered his position by referring to World War II aerial bombardment: "All it did was reinforce the enemy's will to resist. This air campaign," he went on, gesturing toward Warden, "maybe there are some interesting things to it, but I don't think that it is right yet."[6]

Loh jumped in before anyone else could respond. "It can be decisive and provide another set of conditions for future action, or if you hit the right set of targeting [you won't need any future actions]."[7] Unfortunately, everyone at the table then began talking about the simultaneous execution of Instant Thunder and a yet-to-be-devised land campaign—precisely the discussion Alexander and Loh sought to avoid. Warden, Loh, and Alexander argued against the idea of simultaneous execution. Even Butler, who up to this time had said little, sided with Warden and the others. It was Admiral Jeremiah, though, who managed to get the discussion back on track.

"What if you flow [forces and equipment] for the strategic air campaign and *then* flow for land operations?"[8] asked Jeremiah. That seemed to make sense to everyone, including Chairman Powell.

"Once you've done strategic," said Powell, "you don't want to leave Hiroshima and then wait for results."[9]

"Make sure operations to achieve tactical-level objectives don't compromise success of the strategic air campaign!" cautioned Alexander, his voice rising over the din caused by everyone talking at the same time.

Powell waved him aside. "Right, but I can't recommend only the strategic air campaign to the president. The campaign I laid out for the president was sweep the air, leave the tanks to be picked off piecemeal. Make it joint."[10] Because Powell focused on broader matters than anyone else at the table, he was concerned about everything.

"When can we execute the strategic air campaign if we do not alter the flow plan?" asked Butler.

"We don't know,"[11] said Warden candidly. He and the other planners had spent hours discussing the flow and had high hopes that this meeting would convince Powell to put pressure on the supporting CINCs to flow what was really needed to make Instant Thunder work.

Powell furrowed his brow and laid his military-issue reading glasses on the table. "The strategic air campaign appears ordnance-limited vice airplane-limited."

"Tankers could be a limitation," said Loh. "We have already done some initial excursions and [have seen] we are going to need more tankers."[12]

"Come back and talk to me and to CINCCENT [commander in chief, Central Command] on the logistics considerations,"[13] said Powell as he stood up, indicating that the meeting was over. "We have to get a 15-to-20-minute version of the briefing. I need about five slides to brief the SECDEF."[14] Powell picked up his notes and walked out the door. The others followed soon after.

Warden and the rest of the Air Force people in attendance followed General Loh to his fourth-floor office to review the tasking that had come out of the meeting. Loh realized that Powell's mandate to kill Iraqi armor would require what amounted to a two-phase plan: first, the strategic air campaign and then the systematic destruction of Saddam's tanks and armored personnel carriers (APC) from the air. The vice-chief told the group that, by nightfall, he wanted 15 good slides from which Powell could select the five he needed to brief the SECDEF. In addition, Loh wanted Warden's people to take a hard look at tanker and munitions limitations as they applied to the execution of Instant Thunder. As the plan evolved from a concept into an executable war-fighting operation, these kinds of shortfalls could spell disaster unless the planners recognized them early. The big thing, General Loh reminded the group, was that they needed to do everything in the name of the CINC (i.e., Schwarzkopf) and not the Air Force. The operation had to be joint from head to toe, or it wouldn't fly.

At 1130 colonels Bigelow, Bristow, and Hawkins—sent by TAC to help with air campaign planning—arrived at the Pentagon and made their way down to the Checkmate facility. Warden greeted the men enthusiastically and ushered them inside. He knew from discussions with Alexander and Loh that TAC's nose was still a little out of joint over the Instant Thunder plan, and he wanted to do his best to quickly incorporate these colonels into the planning process.[15] It wasn't going to be easy.

"Look, did you get a copy of the things that were faxed up here from TAC concerning General Russ's concerns?" asked Dick Bigelow as he swung his padlocked briefcase onto a nearby table.

Warden hesitated a split second. "Yes, we did, but it has been decided not to use that."[16] The three colonels looked at one another and then back at Warden. He led them into a small conference area and gave them a detailed briefing on the Instant Thunder plan and its development. They weren't anymore impressed with the plan now than when they first took it off the fax machine at Langley two days ago.

Hawkins, a high-strung, dark-haired man of medium build with thin lips and very pale skin, was the first to speak. "There is a big flaw in what you are doing," he said nervously. "If it is an all-out campaign to win, you cannot forget about the combat power/combat strength which is massed in Kuwait, which can move south and take a lot of the northern-tier bases in Saudi and actually could move as far south as Riyadh!"[17] Warden dismissed that scenario as highly unlikely. The main effort, he told them, was the strategic air campaign against Iraq itself.

"You can't just go bomb Iraq and expect to win," countered Bristow, the tallest and quietest of the three TAC colonels. He had dealt with Warden on other issues in the past and knew full well how he operated. "You've got to consider the threat along the Iraqi border!"[18] Warden disagreed and explained his position all over again, adding that both the CINC and now the chairman were in agreement that the Instant Thunder plan was a sound approach to the current crisis—they merely had

75

to expand it. Furthermore, Warden informed the group, the plan had to be ready to meet an execution date of 3 September. The TAC colonels were speechless. They had no idea things had moved so quickly. Just last night they had sat in General Russ's study and received their marching orders. Surely someone would have told Russ about changes as sweeping as these!

Stunned, Bristow excused himself as Warden assigned each TAC colonel to a different planning group, depending on his interest and expertise. Bristow was amazed at the level of activity around him. Everywhere he looked, people were making calls and writing on boards. The main door to the vault area opened every few minutes, and another new face came through and disappeared into one of the cubbyholes that lined the corridors in the Checkmate area. As Bristow walked past what had recently served as the Checkmate bar,* he saw at least 10 intelligence personnel working furiously on target folders. They were part of Col Jim Blackburn's group that had arrived the day before from the Air Force Intelligence Agency (AFIA). After much foot-dragging on the part of Blackburn, AFIA's director of targets, Warden had finally persuaded him to move from his permanent location across the river at Bolling AFB to the Checkmate basement. Now, thick reams of computer printouts and hundreds of rolls of microfiche known as automated tactical target graphics (ATTG)—all belonging to Blackburn's staff—were piled on top of the bar and scattered on tables. People were plugging in highly classified computers that were adrift in a tangle of cables and power cords.[19] Bristow stepped around the mess and made his way down the hall. Soon he found an unused secure phone on the far side of a large, dilapidated planning room. Yellow paint, long since faded to gray, was caked on the walls. The tile floor was stained and covered with scuff marks from carelessly moved desks and chairs. He had no real privacy here, but people were too busy to notice him.

---

*Fighter squadrons typically have a bar or break area somewhere in the unit. After duty hours, pilots gather there to drink and discuss the day's flying. Since many fighter pilots worked in Checkmate, a bar was set aside for their use.

Bristow dialed General Griffith's office and, once he got the general on the line, waited for the phones to synchronize into the secure mode. When "Top Secret, Langley AFB VA" flashed on his receiver, Bristow started talking.

"Sir, the basic tenets that you submitted—the concept that came from TAC and General Russ—we have been told [that they] have been looked at and disregarded. They are pressing on with the basic plan that you saw yesterday. They are going to make some minor applications [sic] to it." A long pause ensued. For a minute, Bristow thought the line might have dropped off. "By the way," said Bristow, his voice rising slightly in pitch as the machine scrambled his words and sent them to Langley, "the execution date is 3 September."

"You've got to be [expletive deleted] me!" choked Griffith.

"No, sir," said Bristow, his heart pounding. "That is what we are working towards . . . an early September execution."

"Keep me informed, and give me a call back tonight before you guys go home."[20]

Bristow hung up, and the small screen on the receiver flashed several times, indicating he had exited the secure mode. He looked around the room, wondering if anyone had overheard his conversation with Griffith. It didn't matter. The colonel had every right to keep TAC informed. The people up here certainly didn't seem interested in doing that.

Sun/12 Aug 90/Pentagon/Wash DC

As Lt Gen Jimmie Adams made his way up the wide steps of the Pentagon's River Entrance, he could scarcely control his rage. It wasn't the fact that his long-anticipated visit to Disney World with his wife and grandson had been cut short by the Iraqi invasion. What piqued him were the actions of a particularly onerous staff officer—Col John A. Warden III. For the first few days of his vacation, he stayed in touch with his office using a secure phone installed in his VOQ room at Patrick AFB, Florida, but his deputy, General May, soon convinced him that Warden and the group he had assembled in Checkmate were getting out of control.[21] On Friday morning, Adams packed up, left Patrick, and drove to Atlanta, where he dropped off his grandson. The next day, he made the grueling, 14-hour drive back to Washington. To make matters worse, he had barely settled down in his quarters at Bolling Saturday night when the phone rang. It was General Loh. The vice-chief wanted him to come over to his quarters at Bolling next morning for a breakfast meeting to discuss what they needed to do with the planning effort Alexander and Warden had started. Adams was not at all certain what had transpired since he left Patrick, but he was not about to let the vice-chief know that. After he finished talking with Loh, Adams started making a flurry of phone calls to try to find out. What he learned did not make him happy.

The heavy, wooden, automatic doors at the top of the Pentagon's River Entrance swung open, and General Adams walked through. It was only a little after seven in the morning, but already the inner corridor felt cool compared to the hot, moisture-laden air outside. He showed his pass to the security guard, who ushered him into the marble hall. General Alexander was waiting for him, briefcase in hand. Apprehensive about what Adams might say and do, the plans director didn't look at all well. He had spent most of last evening at the Pentagon along with General May. Both men, upon learning that Adams was cutting his vacation short, had expected to see him that night. May waited until about 2000 hours and finally went home. Alexander stayed even later. Neither officer dreamed that Adams would drive all the way back from Florida instead of catching a plane. None of that mattered now. Alexander and Adams were face-to-face.

They walked behind the main corridor that led directly to the chairman's office and stood in a quiet, half-lit anteroom, discussing the events of the past few days. Alexander looked around before he opened the leather briefcase and showed Adams the Instant Thunder slides inside. As his boss flipped through the material, Alexander casually mentioned that he had reviewed the same slides with General Butler earlier that morning. Adams turned on Alexander with a fury. He excoriated the two-star for letting everything go in the wrong direction. Warden was out of control again, and Alexander was to blame. The painful silence that followed was broken only by Adams muttering under his breath as he looked at each of the remaining slides. He shoved them back into the briefcase and motioned for Alexander to close it.[22] In a hiss that could be heard throughout the adjacent corridors, Adams let Alexander know that he had no confidence in the plan. It reminded him too much of Vietnam.[23] Before dismissing the now thoroughly shaken Alexander, Adams told him he was no longer needed on the project. Adams would take control of it himself. He stomped up the stairs and headed for his office, determined to call Lt Col Foose Wilson the first chance he got. Adams needed someone he could trust* to help clean up the mess that Warden and Alexander had created.

Around 0930 Adams threw the stack of papers he had been working on into his out basket and headed for General Loh's quarters and the breakfast meeting he'd been ordered to attend. Because Bolling was just a short drive from the Pentagon and Sunday traffic was light, Adams reached the quiet, tree-lined street known as "generals' row" within minutes. He parked the car, leaving the windows down, and made his way up the flowered path to Loh's residence. The beauty and order of the modest but impeccably maintained house and grounds seemed completely out of synch with Adams's mood. General Carns had arrived earlier, and both he and Loh were already at the breakfast table when Adams walked in. They got right down to business.

Loh explained that Schwarzkopf had tasked him to put together an air campaign. In order to do that and make it joint, as the chairman requested, he needed some way to make Adams, who was the Air Force operations deputy, a legitimate representative of the Joint Staff. "We need you to be the air guy, the air planner for the air campaign,"[24] said Loh, pointing his coffee spoon at Adams. Loh was concerned that Lt Gen Tom Kelly would dominate the whole process and drastically diminish the contribution air could make to Schwarzkopf's campaign. He didn't want that to happen, and neither did Carns. Both men agreed to make Jimmie Adams the "deputy J-3 for air."[25] This "official" title would help smooth any ruffled

---

*A member of the Fighter Mafia, Wilson was one of the few officers in operations who had worked for both Adams and Horner. Adams was confident that Wilson had not and would not be co-opted by Warden and his followers.

feathers in the JCS and elsewhere over concerns about Air Force involvement in the CINC's planning. Carns was certain that Lee Butler would agree to this approach and that even Kelly would probably buy it for the time being. It was worth a try.

Adams got in his car and drove back to the Pentagon, his head swimming with the huge and unwelcome task that General Loh had suddenly thrust upon him. [expletive deleted], the last thing he wanted to do was get involved in Chuck Horner's and CENTCOM's business! [expletive deleted] John Warden and his ivory tower ideas about air power! He sped past the old, deserted Pentagon boat-docking area with its rows upon rows of brightly colored geraniums and pansies, where, years ago, a ferryboat delivered its daily cargo of Pentagon employees who commuted to work from Bolling AFB. Adams pulled into his parking slot at the River Entrance and made his way inside. He took the poorly lit stairs at the left of the marble and mahogany corridor and descended to the floors below.

The basement of the Pentagon is unlike anything the Washington visitors see on their carefully guided tours through one of the world's largest office buildings. Open cables hang haphazardly throughout the rambling, underground labyrinth, and on the wider walkways, propane-powered forklifts, laden with huge pallets of books and supplies, roar by, catching the unwary pedestrian by surprise. The Pentagon room-numbering system, so efficient and relatively easy to understand on the other floors, didn't apply in the controlled chaos of the basement. Adams swung past the freight elevators and empty dustbins, heading for the purple water fountain at the end of the corridor. There, he turned right and pushed the entry bell at the Checkmate entrance.

Maj Gen Jim Meier, a JCS officer assigned to the J-3, opened the door and let him inside. Meier explained that he and about 50 other joint officers were now involved in the planning, having been recruited the day before when Powell ordered the effort to become joint. This revelation did little for Adams's mood or blood pressure. After Warden and a sheepish-looking Alexander led him to a briefing room where all the other people had already assembled, they invited the three-star to sit down and review the latest iterations of the Instant Thunder plan.

Adams took a seat and looked at a room swirling with maps, charts, and people from all services. He watched as Warden took some slides from one of his assistants, Lt Col Ron Stanfill, and fairly skipped his way over to the Vu-Graph machine. He seemed almost gleeful, shuffling through the charts, pulling some out, and adding others in preparation for the briefing. The longer Adams watched him, the angrier he got. Soon his hands were shaking, and a hot, red flush made its way from his neck to his face. Warden started talking, and—almost immediately—Adams cut him off, his voice quivering, "I want to see the radio frequencies you are planning to use!"[26] Warden was not prepared to do that. His focus, unlike Adams's, was on the macro process. Frequencies and other minutiae would come later. The colonel was certain that Adams intended to discredit the plan before he even had a chance to show it to him.[27] No doubt Adams's friends at TAC, including General Russ, had told him all sorts of negative things. He wished that Alexander had never faxed the plan to Langley—at least not as early as he had.

"We're not really quite down to radio frequencies," said Warden in a soft, reassuring voice that masked his own anger. "We probably won't get that for you, but let me sort of start at the top and kind of review for you where we are and what the ideas were."[28]

Adams slumped down in his chair and motioned for Warden to continue. The colonel ran through his entire pitch in about 30 minutes, explaining Schwarzkopf's and Powell's reactions to the plan as well as the instructions he had received from Loh and Dugan. By this time, Adams had cooled down a little. No fool, the operations deputy fully understood the implications of the plan's tacit approval by the CINC, the chairman, and his own Air Force bosses. Still, Adams had serious reservations about the plan and didn't hesitate to voice them.

He told the group that, overall, they had done a good job and that he understood their tasking. However, he saw the air campaign as a unilateral effort—one that called for the takedown of Saddam Hussein but ignored the Iraqi troops poised on the Saudi borders. If Adams were to have any confidence in the plan, Warden and his people would have to factor in real-world details on targeting and weaponeering.

Further, he ordered Warden to drop the "six-to-nine-day" air campaign slide, believing that such a prediction served no useful purpose. The bombshell came when Adams stood up and told the assembled group that the plan should focus on destroying the Iraqi army and use whatever assets were left for the strategic air campaign.[29] Warden, who up to now had been low-key and almost conciliatory, shot back, "That's a reversal of what the chairman of the joint chiefs said!"[30] General Meier, who had said nothing during Adams's earlier tirade, agreed with Warden and spoke in his defense. He too understood that the strategic air campaign had first priority and that it would precede any ground campaign. But Adams would not relent, believing that the chairman and the CINC intended to rid Kuwait of Iraqi ground forces in the second phase of Instant Thunder. Warden countered with a blow-by-blow description of his Saturday morning repartee with General Powell.

Determined not to let Warden think he could manage the air war from the Pentagon, Adams growled, "We're not writing frags [fragmentary orders*] in the Pentagon. I learned that seven years ago."[31]

Adams's persistent chipping away at the Instant Thunder plan took a toll on the normally very civilized and correct John Warden. Without thinking, he blurted out, "We don't want to do a half-assed strategic campaign!"

"Right," said Adams, walking up to the map displays and putting his hand over Kuwait. "But we don't want to leave those Iraqi forces in place to kill 200,000 soldiers [either]."[32]

The conversation degenerated into a lengthy discussion about logistics shortfalls and the effort needed to accomplish General Powell's mandate to include a tank-killing phase in the plan. Adams wanted to see a much.expanded, detailed version of Instant Thunder that addressed enemy capabilities, logistics considerations, and tanker support. He wondered aloud if Horner had seen any of this. Colonel Bristow piped up that he had faxed it to the general three days ago. Warden stared at Bristow, who appeared delighted to have been able to give that tidbit of information to General Adams. Walking to the center of the room, Warden cleared his throat and

---

*A flying unit's portion of the air tasking order (ATO).

reminded Bristow that what he faxed to Horner three days ago was nothing more than a bare-bones draft of an early Instant Thunder plan. The version they were working on today was much bigger and—more importantly—had the endorsement of both the CINC and the CJCS.

Sun/12 Aug 90/Mount Vernon VA

Lt Col Foose Wilson had taken leave so he could spend all day Saturday shepherding his mother and father around Washington. Neither had been to the capital before, and they were enjoying the sights and their son's company. Today was especially good. The warm Sunday sunshine was pleasant and far less intense than what they were used to back home in Alabama. The three of them spent the morning poking around George Washington's country estate at Mount Vernon, where the crowds that day were small and unobtrusive. They toured the house and grounds and, after a few hours, made their way to the large wicker and hickory rockers that lined the house's back porch. The chairs were painted authentic colonial black, rubbed bare in spots over the years by footsore tourists like Mrs Wilson, who sat between the men, grateful for a place to rest. For a long while, they rocked in silence, admiring the rich green hills and pastureland that arched its way down to the wide river below.

Foose was contemplating a leisurely lunch when he faintly heard his name called over the public address system: "Colonel Wilson, come to the front gate. There is a military message for you."[33] Wilson excused himself and ambled down the winding path that led from the house to the main entrance. Strange that anyone in his office would need him so desperately on a Sunday afternoon. He was a staff puke, and no one tracked staff pukes down—not all the way to Mount Vernon on a Sunday afternoon! Maybe the war had started!

Wilson knocked on the window of the whitewashed kiosk at the main entrance to Mount Vernon. After he identified himself, a park ranger invited him into the cramped little building and directed him to an open phone that rested on what was left of the *Washington Post* sports pages. Wilson lifted the receiver and found himself talking to Maj Gen Marvin S. Ervin, the Air Force deputy director of operations. He told Wilson that Gen Jimmie Adams needed to see him immediately and that they were sending a government car out to Mount Vernon to pick him up and take him directly to Adams's house on Bolling AFB.

Wilson was dismayed by the prospect of leaving his folks at Mount Vernon and telling them they had to find their way back to his house in the Virginia suburbs. Not only were the roads too complicated, but his sudden departure would cause his parents undue worry. Wilson thought fast. He would take them home himself; that was the simplest, cleanest thing to do. Wilson told General Ervin to send the car to his house instead of Mount Vernon. He would meet the driver there. Reluctantly, Ervin agreed. Foose hung up the phone, thanked the park ranger—who had been staring at him throughout his conversation—and hurried out the door and up the path to rejoin his mother and father.

Sun/12 Aug 90/Bolling AFB/Wash DC

It was almost 1400 when the battered, gunmetal-gray sedan carrying Foose Wilson pulled up in front of General Adams's quarters. Adams lived on the back side of Bolling, not far from the Officers' Club, in one of the brick-and-mortar depression-era houses reserved for general officers who worked at the Pentagon. As soon as Wilson stepped out of the car, he knew something big was up. Adams was standing at his front door, wearing an aloha shirt and shorts, as well as a pained expression on his face—as if he'd just heard that his best friend had died. The general ushered Wilson inside, patting him gently on the shoulder, saying, "Steve, I have a mission for you."[34] Adams explained that he had spoken earlier in the day with General Horner about the planning being done at the Air Staff and that Horner was unhappy because it had occurred without his knowledge or consent. Horner needed to know exactly what was happening in Washington and how it might affect his operation in Riyadh—and he needed to know soon. Adams had chosen Wilson to tell him.

"There are going to be a lot of spears thrown," warned Adams. "There will be a lot of people asking a lot of questions, and [Horner] will yell a lot. He will bark a lot. He will appear not to listen, but he will listen."[35]

None of this came as a surprise to Wilson, who remembered interviewing with Horner for a squadron commander position in one of the general's fighter units. He had screamed at him just like his dad used to. Wilson knew that underneath his gruffness, Horner had a soft heart. The trick was to play along with him—just listen, be respectful, and keep going. It had worked for Wilson. Horner hired him that very day.[36]

Within the hour, both men were on their way to see General Loh. At that meeting, Adams did most of the talking, reiterating to Loh his earlier conversation with General Horner and his intention to send Foose Wilson over to Riyadh to help defuse the situation. Loh listened impassively, adding nothing. Adams quickly excused himself and left with Wilson in tow.

Their next stop was the command center, where Wilson was subjected to what seemed like endless briefings on highly classified programs.[37] Adams was making Wilson drink out of a fire hose, and Foose really didn't understand why! But later that afternoon, as he sat in the Checkmate area listening to Deptula and Warden describing Instant Thunder for the 10th time and thinking that he couldn't possibly get enough information to be comfortable briefing Horner, it dawned on him that they actually intended for him to leave that night! Adams seriously expected him to jump on a plane and head to the desert. He hadn't even packed, yet they were talking about airplanes ready to move him in the next couple of hours. Adams had left the building, but Wilson found out where he was and telephoned him.

"I can't leave until tomorrow morning," said Wilson matter-of-factly. "I need more briefings, and I need more time to pack and get ready."[38]

It didn't take much coaxing for Adams to relent and allow Wilson the additional time he needed—it simply made sense. Relieved, Wilson hung up and continued talking with Deptula and some of the members of his own fighter shop who were down in Checkmate helping with targeting and munitions selection. He left near midnight, his head swimming with Instant Thunder facts and figures.

Mon/13 Aug 90/Pentagon/Wash DC

By 0500 Wilson was back in the Checkmate area, where he picked up the latest iteration of Instant Thunder and its target list from Warden and Dave Deptula. Both men had been working frantically on those documents. He also took all the supporting top secret and special access required (SAR) data his briefcase would hold. Loaded down with his travel bag and the special courier briefcase that attached to his wrist with a lock and key, Wilson walked out the River Entrance at 0800 and stepped into a waiting government car that would take him to Dover, Delaware—the first leg of his long journey to Riyadh.[39]

Wilson slumped down in the back seat of the cramped government car and tried to get some rest. It was no use. No matter how he contorted himself, he couldn't find a comfortable position. The briefcase tugged at his arm, and the sharp plastic door handles on the cheap, compact car dug into his sides, making sleep impossible. Reluctantly, he sat up and watched the scenery. Leaving Washington was very slow going. The late summer sun beat down on the snarl of busses, trucks, and cars creeping up the Baltimore-Washington Parkway, making Wilson's ride even more unpleasant. Occasionally, a motorcycle roared past, startling Foose and his driver as the T-shirted biker wove his machine at unbelievable speeds between the long lines of frustrated drivers. Gradually, however, the traffic eased, and in a few hours Wilson found himself in the open farmland that stretches from the Chesapeake to Dover.

Mon/13 Aug 90/Dover AFB DE

The people at Dover AFB were expecting him—at least that's how it appeared to Wilson. As soon as he arrived, they waved him onto a waiting C-5 Galaxy, jammed to the rafters with Army troops and equipment. The lieutenant colonel tried to climb up the steep ladder from the cargo compartment to the troop deck, but his briefcase kept getting stuck in the narrow ladder. He had to hold it back with his left hand and steady himself on the ladder with his right. Finally, he made it "up top," looked around for a seat, and discovered they were all occupied by wide-eyed 82d Airborne rangers loaded down with combat gear and assault weapons. The crew chief—a grizzled reservist—motioned for Wilson to follow him back down the ladder. For a minute, Wilson thought he was going to throw him off the plane; instead, the sergeant took him on a winding journey through a maze of pallets and vehicles to the front of the aircraft. Briefcase in hand, Wilson banged his way up another flight of stairs that, thankfully, led to the C-5's cockpit. Inside, the crew chief gave Wilson a terse smile and pointed to a vacant jump seat. Wilson had no sooner sat down than the aircraft started to move, its engines straining under the heavy load. Several minutes later, when the C-5 rolled to a stop at the departure end of the runway, the two pilots turned around and stared briefly at Wilson, as if to confirm that it really was a lousy lieutenant colonel that they had been ordered to wait for. Satisfied, they turned their attention back to the mission at hand, and soon the huge bird lumbered down the heat-soaked runway and struggled into the air. As the biggest aircraft in the Air Force inventory slowly gained speed and altitude, it swung north past a thousand towns, small and large, before it reluctantly turned east and headed out to sea.

Mon/13 Aug 90/Ramstein AB, Germany

Eight hours later, the cargo jet swooped low over the darkened countryside, flaps fully extended, wheels down, and engines making an awful droning sound as the Volkswagen-sized compressor blades cut their way through the thick, Teutonic air toward an uneventful landing at Ramstein Air Base. The C-5 did a high-speed taxi to the deserted, far side of the base—normally reserved for handling dangerous cargo and special missions. The crew door opened, and light from the interior of the plane streamed onto the taxiway, illuminating a small contingent of heavily armed security police. A solitary figure emerged from the plane, stepped out into the cool, night air, and hurried over to where the police were waiting. The men saluted, and Wilson—despite fatigue and the weight of his omnipresent briefcase—managed to raise his right hand crisply to forehead. The group turned and watched as the aircraft slowly pivoted and headed back toward the passenger terminal, a half mile distant.

The three men who had joined Wilson on the darkened taxiway said little but kept stealing furtive glances at the buff-colored briefcase still firmly attached to his wrist. Two of the policemen were barely out of their teens—one still wore a retainer. The third, eight stripes showing on his camouflaged sleeve, was by far the senior member of the group. He motioned for Wilson to get into the back of the police car with him, while the other two men clambered into the front, their automatic weapons at the ready.

They drove only a short distance before Wilson could see the distinctive outline of a green and gray camouflaged C-5, engines running. Noticing that the tail number on this transport was different than the one he had come over on, Wilson thought it must be his new ride. Sure enough, the squad car stopped just beyond the giant aircraft's wingtip, and all four men got out. As they did, the lower hatch swung open and the crew chief appeared, motioning Wilson to come aboard. The young policeman with the retainer accompanied Wilson to the plane, carrying his hang-up bag and suitcase. The other two men kept watch a discreet distance away, their faces ghostly pale in the blue light of the squad car. As soon as the young airman passed Wilson's bag to him, the crew hatch began to close, and Wilson barely had enough time to grunt out thanks to the disappearing image of the security cop's polished boots. Minutes later, the C-5 roared down the runway and lifted off into the clear night sky.

Tue/14 Aug 90/Dhahran, Saudi Arabia

Stepping off the airlifter, Wilson saw nothing but planes, people, and shimmering waves of heat. Insufferable heat, the kind that settles on your chest and neck, threatening to push you feet first through the tarmac and into the powder-fine sand that stretched to the horizon. Sand was everywhere, working its way into your clothing, up your nose, and in your eyes. You breathed it, ate it, and drank it. The C-5 pilot who escorted Wilson over to the C-21A Learjet detachment told him that if you stayed in Saudi long enough, you began to think you were made of it. As they walked toward a small hangar, Wilson was amazed by the sheer numbers of soldiers, all from the 82d Airborne, camped along the taxiways and wedged into any area that could provide shelter from the broiling midday heat.[40] The whole place seemed like something out of a movie set.

Wilson was starving. He hadn't eaten anything since leaving Dover almost 18 hours ago. The C-21A crew—huddled in a corner of a huge hangar crawling with troops and cargo—proved friendly enough, offering to take him to dinner before they carried him on the last leg of his journey to Riyadh. Sitting in a makeshift diner, gulping down a warm Coke and a greasy burger, Wilson had to admit that General Ervin, the Air Force Command Center guru, really knew his stuff. He had traveled almost 14,000 miles on the travel plan coordinated by Ervin through the airlift control element (ACE) at the Pentagon without so much as a set of orders![41] Waiting airplanes and welcoming aircrews were all part of Ervin's well-established connections with Military Airlift Command (MAC).* Later that afternoon, as he made his way back out to the flight line for the ride to Riyadh, Wilson wasn't sure whether his sudden nausea stemmed from the hamburger or the prospect of briefing General Horner. Time would tell.

Tue/14 Aug 90/Riyadh, Saudi Arabia

By the time Wilson's plane landed at Riyadh, it was already dark. He thanked the crew for their hospitality and hitched a ride to Royal Saudi Air Force (RSAF) headquarters. Once inside the building, Foose made his way to the office of

---

*Replaced by Air Mobility Command (AMC) in 1992.

Maj Gen Tom Olsen, deputy commander of CENTAF, who was handling most of the problems while Horner served as the on-scene CENTCOM commander.* Feeling a bit awkward, Wilson explained the reason for his visit. He knew that even though Olsen and the others welcomed him to the theater as an old fighter buddy, they harbored serious resentment about what the rumor mill told them—that he was meddling in the theater commander's business by bringing a campaign plan built by the Air Staff.[42] Wilson slid the key into the bracelet that held the briefcase to his arm and opened the lock. The briefcase fell away with a thud and dropped beside his feet. As he reached down to open it for the first time since leaving the Pentagon, he noticed that his flight boots were covered with a light dusting of sand. Wilson pulled out a sealed manila envelope marked "TOP SECRET LIMDIS [limited distribution]" and placed it on the table. He carefully opened it and pulled out the Instant Thunder plan and its targeting list.

Olsen was quite congenial as Colonel Wilson walked him through the briefing. The general interrupted him at one point to summon his director of operations, Col Jim Crigger, a veteran fighter pilot who, before the war was over, would manage to fly an impressive number of combat sorties in F-15C/D Eagle air superiority fighters. For now, though, Crigger was consumed with the beddown of CENTAF assets and the frantic efforts of his staff to put together a defensive plan just in case Saddam's forces rolled south into Saudi Arabia.[43] Like his boss, Crigger had very few questions about Instant Thunder. This surprised Wilson because he had expected them both to pepper him with questions and comments on everything from tactics to targets, dissecting each aiming point and arguing over the best aircraft for the job. Yet, neither man said much of anything.[44] They were polite and pleasant enough, but Olsen and his deputy conveyed the unmistakable impression that they weren't very interested in what Wilson and the Air Staff had to offer.

After Wilson put the top secret slides back in the briefcase, Crigger called in his weapons officer, Lt Col Sam Baptiste. Wilson and Baptiste were old friends whose paths had crossed

_____
*General Schwarzkopf was still in Florida at this time.

many times in their various assignments as Eagle jet drivers. Olsen told Baptiste to accompany Wilson over to Headquarters CENTCOM and view the briefing there with General Horner.

"You take my car and driver," said Olsen. "Go see Horner."[45]

Headquarters CENTCOM was a four-mile drive from the RSAF compound. The streets were alive with military trucks and busses and an odd assortment of American and German cars driven by stern-looking Arab men. After they arrived at the headquarters, Wilson and Baptiste were kept waiting almost an hour. It was all part of the game.[46] Actually, Foose was surprised and grateful that they were ushered into the commander's office so quickly. He had expected Horner to make them wait all night. Soon, he would wish they had.

Wilson and Baptiste had barely stepped through the doorway and into the huge, opulently furnished room that served as Horner's temporary office, when Wilson's old boss, fury in his eyes, began flaying him alive. Before Wilson could say a word, Horner told him that he understood why he was there and, more importantly, what he had.[47] The general strode angrily across the room and looked down at Wilson, his eyes bulging and his lips pulled back in a sneer. Grabbing Foose's tie, he told him in no uncertain terms that it wasn't Wilson's job—or anybody else's on the Air Staff—to plan an air campaign.[48] For a split second, it looked like Horner was going to hit him. The colonel winced as the general tightened his grip on the tie and pulled him closer. Instead of smashing the wiry, handsome colonel with his fist, Horner hissed out a warning that it wasn't Wilson's job to push this plan down CENTAF's throat.[49]

After the harangue was over and Horner had made his objections, he let Wilson open his briefcase and take out the envelope containing the Instant Thunder material. No sooner had Wilson pulled out the first slide than Horner picked it up and tossed it across the room. It hit the wall with a thunk and fluttered soundlessly down onto a brightly colored Persian rug. In a voice louder than normal but still controlled, Horner told Wilson that he hated the term *Instant Thunder*, so Wilson shouldn't have used it. The general then fired off a series of questions: How did he arrive at that term? Who gave the plan that name? Was Warden in on the planning? Why did Wilson call it Instant Thunder?[50]

The colonel tried his best to answer, but Horner was not in a listening mode—he was all transmit. Finally, Wilson gathered up the slides that Horner had thrown around the room and told the general that he could do this over and over, but the bottom line was that Gen H. Norman Schwarzkopf, Horner's boss, had requested this plan and that Wilson's boss, Gen John M. Loh, had told him to deliver it, and that was what he was going to do![51]

Wilson set up the slides and went through each one, just as he had rehearsed with Deptula and Warden. This time, Horner sat quietly, arms folded, muttering under his breath only when something struck him as especially stupid. "I'm not worried about strategic targets," he told Wilson. To the general, strategic targeting meant *nuclear* targeting, and Gen Chuck Horner was not going nuclear. His concern was the Iraqi army assembled along the Kuwaiti-Saudi border. Horner was convinced that Saddam intended to send it into Saudi Arabia to take control of the ports and oil.[52]

After the briefing, Horner seemed calmer and more himself. He admitted being frustrated over his boss's request to the Air Staff, adding that Schwarzkopf simply didn't know what he was asking for and that it wasn't his job to ask outsiders for an air campaign in the first place! As far as Horner was concerned, *he* was the only one Schwarzkopf should have tasked with building an air campaign! After all, he was the CENTAF commander![53]

As Wilson gathered up his things and prepared to go, Horner asked him when he was headed back to the States. "Tomorrow," Wilson told him. Horner smiled slyly and, as he walked back to his desk, casually commented that Wilson had better think again—he was going to be there a while. Wilson stopped packing and looked up at the general. "I don't work for you."

"Yes," said Horner, gravel in his voice, "General Loh says you work for me, and you are here to help."[54]

Horner wanted Wilson to stay long enough to get the intelligence information lines flowing in CENTAF. The targeting photos and data Wilson brought with him to illustrate the briefing were better than anything Horner had seen in-theater—just what the general wanted. He told Wilson to get in touch with his CIA and DIA contacts back in

Washington and have them open up the intelligence channels. Patting Foose on the back, the general told him that he would have a work area right next door to his in the RSAF headquarters. Currently, three one-stars occupied it, but Horner was confident they wouldn't mind sharing a little of their space with Wilson. Dumbfounded, Wilson stumbled out the door and followed Baptiste down the stairs and out into the night. His whole body felt numb, and he was too tired to carry on much of a conversation with his friend. As Baptiste dumped him into a hotel room, Wilson noted that his old look'em-in-the-eye fighter buddy hadn't said much during the Horner meeting—nothing much at all.[55] As Wilson dozed off, half a world away, the president of the United States was getting his first look at the Instant Thunder plan. He would like it a lot more than General Horner did.

Notes

1. Lt Gen Robert M. Alexander, Washington, D.C., transcript of interview with Lt Col Suzanne B. Gehri, Lt Col Edward C. Mann, and author, 30 May 1991, 33, Desert Story Collection, US Air Force Historical Research Agency, Maxwell AFB, Ala.

2. Ibid., 19, 33–34.

3. Ibid., 34.

4. Col John A. Warden III, Washington, D.C., transcript of interview with Lt Col Suzanne B. Gehri, Lt Col Edward C. Mann, and author, 30 May 1991, 99, Desert Story Collection, US Air Force Historical Research Agency, Maxwell AFB, Ala.

5. Alexander, 30 May 1991, 36.

6. Gen John M. Loh, Langley AFB, Va., transcript of interview with Lt Col Suzanne B. Gehri and author, 26 September 1991, 20, Desert Story Collection, US Air Force Historical Research Agency, Maxwell AFB, Ala.

7. Ibid.

8. Alexander, 30 May 1991, 36.

9. Notes, Lt Col Ben Harvey, 23, Desert Story Collection, US Air Force Historical Research Agency, Maxwell AFB, Ala. (Secret) Information extracted here and in subsequent references is unclassified. Hereinafter referred to as Harvey.

10. Alexander, 30 May 1991, 36, 40.

11. Ibid., 37.

12. Ibid.

13. Ibid., 38.

14. Ibid., 32; and Harvey, 24.

15. Harvey, 25.

16. Col Richard D. Bristow, Langley AFB, Va., transcript of interview with Lt Col Edward C. Mann and author, 9 November 1992, 21–22, Desert Story Collection, US Air Force Historical Research Agency, Maxwell AFB, Ala.

17. Ibid.

18. Ibid., 22–23.

19. Col James Blackburn, Bolling AFB, Washington, D.C., transcript of interview with Lt Col Suzanne B. Gehri, Col Edward C. Mann, and author, 21 April 1993, 21–26, Desert Story Collection, US Air Force Historical Research Agency, Maxwell AFB, Ala.

20. Bristow, 9 November 1992, 25.

21. Gen Jimmie V. Adams, Eglin AFB, Fla., transcript of interview with Lt Col Suzanne B. Gehri and author, 3 February 1992, 1–3, Desert Story Collection, US Air Force Historical Research Agency, Maxwell AFB, Ala.

22. Harvey, 29.

23. Ibid.

24. Loh, 26 September 1991, 22.

25. Ibid., 24.

26. Warden, 30 May 1991, 111.

27. Ibid.

28. Ibid.

29. Harvey, 31.

30. Ibid., 31–32.

31. Ibid.

32. Ibid., 32.

33. Col Steve Wilson, Washington, D.C., transcript of interview with Lt Col Suzanne B. Gehri, Lt Col Edward C. Mann, and author, 11 December 1991, 6, Desert Story Collection, US Air Force Historical Research Agency, Maxwell AFB, Ala.

34. Ibid., 6–7.

35. Ibid., 11.

36. Ibid.

37. Ibid.

38. Ibid.

39. Ibid., 12.

40. Ibid., 13.

41. Ibid.

42. Ibid., 14–15.

43. Col James Crigger, Shaw AFB, S.C., transcript of interview with Lt Col Suzanne B. Gehri and author, 3 December 1991, 6, Desert Story Collection, US Air Force Historical Research Agency, Maxwell AFB, Ala.

44. Wilson, 11 December 1991, 15.

45. Ibid.

46. Ibid.

47. Ibid.

48. Ibid.

49. Ibid.

50. Ibid., 16.

51. Ibid., 16–17.

52. Ibid., 17, 20.

53. Ibid., 18.

54. Ibid.

55. Ibid., 16.

Chapter 6

0955/Wed/15 Aug 90/Wash DC

The presidential motorcade pulled up smartly to the River Entrance of the Pentagon. Standing at the bottom of the wide, gray steps that led up to the entrance were Dick Cheney and Colin Powell. Behind them, workers busily put the final touches on the raised platform from which President Bush would address the Pentagon faithful at lunchtime. A VIP seating area had already been fenced off in the parking area to hold the 160 generals and civilian dignitaries who had been invited to hear the speech.[1] The rest of the almost 30,000 Pentagon workers would have to make do, either standing or sitting on the open lawn that stretched for more than 100 yards toward the Potomac River.

After President Bush climbed out of the limousine, Cheney and Powell immediately escorted him up the stairs and into the building. Once inside, the men made their way directly to the briefing area in the tank. Other members of the JCS were already in place, waiting for the presidential party. Powell got right to the point. Using slides given to him by General Loh and General Meier,* the chairman briefed the president on Instant Thunder. During the hour-long meeting, the president asked questions about both the plan and the status of the massive, ongoing military deployment to the Gulf. By the time Bush emerged from the Pentagon to deliver his address at the River Entrance, he was excited—almost vibrant.

"Saddam Hussein would have us believe that his un-provoked invasion of a friendly Arab nation is a struggle between Arabs and Americans," said Bush, looking sternly at the assembled crowd. He paused, gathered himself up, and stabbed at the air with an outstretched finger. "This is clearly false. It is Saddam who lied to his Arab neighbors. It is Saddam who invaded an Arab state. It is Saddam who now

---

*At 1130 on 14 August, General Meier took five slides from the Instant Thunder briefing to General Powell. Later the same day, General Adams said those same slides were going to the president. Harvey, 54, 57 (see note 14).

threatens the Arab nation. We, by contrast, seek to assist our Arab friends in their hour of need."[2] The loudspeakers carried Bush's words across the lawn and down to the river, where they faded away. This was the first time that the president denounced the Iraqi invasion in such harsh, personal terms. It wouldn't be the last.

0530/Fri/17 Aug 90/Andrews AFB MD

Col Dick Bristow pressed his nose to the windshield of the rental car in a vain attempt to see the road ahead. An impenetrable, gray fog blanketed the city and its outlying districts. A perilously overloaded and abused truck, its single working headlight dancing crazily up and down, roared out of the gloom and headed for downtown Washington. Going the other way were empty taxis with tired-looking drivers, their hands draped loosely over the wheel, cigarettes dangling from their mouths. The colonel was grateful he wasn't driving. That task fell to one of the SAC people who had come to help with the planning. The younger officer, looking even more nervous than Bristow, picked his way through the unfamiliar, monochrome landscape toward their destination, Andrews AFB.

Bristow's head ached from lack of sleep and an overwhelming sense of frustration and loss. The other two colonels from TAC had gone home earlier in the week on orders from General Ryan. Bristow suspected that his companions were glad to return to Langley—especially Doug Hawkins, who chafed at the idea of people in Washington putting together an air campaign. It galled him that Warden and the others could get away with building a plan like Instant Thunder behind General Horner's back. The paper-thin excuse that they were acting under the authority and direction of the theater CINC was nonsense. It was wrong—flat-out wrong—to do war planning in Washington, and Hawkins knew it. As far as he was concerned, everyone else should have known it too.

If Bristow hadn't done some quick thinking, he would have returned to Langley with Hawkins and Bigelow. Instead, he persuaded both Ryan and General Griffith that he should accompany the Checkmate group to the meeting with

Schwarzkopf. In order to cut the deal, though, he had to promise to bring back a firsthand account of Schwarzkopf's reaction to the plan, as well as copies of all the material used to brief the CINC. Even so, Bristow's handlers at TAC were none too pleased that he was going.[3]

Bristow closed his eyes and replayed the week's events for the hundredth time. He remembered the shaky start with Colonel Warden on Saturday, 11 August, and the late-night phone call with General Griffith when he asked that some TAC experts be sent to Checkmate to work on weaponeering and other vital planning details. When General Ryan called him early the next morning to tell him that he and Griffith had agreed to that request, Bristow became ecstatic!

Emboldened by Ryan's response, he asked the general if he would mind sending a couple of people from the tactical air control center (TACC) at Ninth Air Force to work on the plan as well. After all, these folks would have to execute the plan, so why not get them involved in putting it together?* Ryan agreed and later arranged to fly two staff officers to Andrews, where Bristow would pick them up the following morning. Later, Bristow casually mentioned to Warden that a couple of guys from Shaw would be up to help work on the plan for a few days before they left for the theater. Warden, knee-deep in paper and ideas, simply nodded. They were in.[4]

The weapons experts showed up on Monday, 13 August, along with the two men from Ninth Air Force. Everyone went right to work, the weapons folks helping various teams determine run-in lines, aiming points, and appropriate munition selections. Bristow shepherded the two Ninth Air Force officers around the various planning cells, explaining as he went exactly what they were trying to accomplish. The level of activity was unbelievable! Warden and some of his key assistants were briefing flag officers from every service on the planning effort. By midafternoon, the Navy had a gaggle of people in the little briefing room, conferring with Dave Deptula and others on how best to use the Tomahawk land attack missile (TLAM) in the Instant Thunder plan.[5]

---

*The TACC at Shaw AFB was preparing to deploy to Saudi Arabia in support of Operation Desert Shield.

That wasn't all. Other services quickly brought in their experts with the latest information on super-secret and not-so-secret weapons and alternatives for their employment. These experts worked with everyone, including the special operations people. The place was also crawling with energetic, excited SAC people, who could be found throughout the Checkmate area, advising on bomb loads, logistics, and weaponeering. What amazed Bristow at the time was that the entire plan to win the war—not just the air war but the *war*—was taking shape in the basement of the Pentagon right before his eyes![6] Planners were systematically filling two four-inch-thick binders—the same ones that Warden would take to Schwarzkopf later in the week—with detailed information on how to fight the war. They had everything from an electronic warfare plan to mean impact points and run-in lines for 84 selected targets. They even had a sample ATO in the works!

Bristow was so excited that he called General Griffith that night. "Sir, you *have got* to come up to Washington and see this because *you just won't believe what is going on!*"[7] Griffith obliged, and on Tuesday morning, 14 August, he flew in by helicopter to the Pentagon. It was the worst thing that could have happened.

Accompanied by Bristow, General Griffith left the helipad and went directly to General Alexander's office, where Alexander greeted him and thanked him for the good services of Bigelow, Hawkins, and Bristow. Secretly, Alexander thought the three men were the biggest nuisance he ever saw. All they wanted to do was spy on the rest of the people and send negative reports back to TAC.[8]

The plans general began by going over the Instant Thunder briefing with Griffith, who was in no mood for a briefing from Alexander or anyone else, for that matter. Besides, he'd already seen the briefing since Hawkins and Bristow had sent a copy to TAC soon after they got to Washington. Unaware of Griffith's frustration, Alexander calmly turned to the second slide.

"Time right now is in [Hussein's] favor,"[9] said Alexander thoughtfully, as he peered at the slide through his reading glasses, which were perilously close to falling off his nose.

Griffith exploded, his face angry and red. He slammed down his fist and pushed his chair away from the conference table, so startling Alexander that he blinked several times in disbelief.

"What do you mean 'time is in [Hussein's] favor'?"[10] shot back Griffith through clenched teeth. "We need the time! We need the time to get our people over and everything else!"[11]

The two men stared at each other for a while, saying nothing. Finally, Alexander flipped a cover sheet over the classified slides and pushed them aside. The briefing was over. For the next few minutes, they talked politely about what and whom Griffith would see during his short stay at the Pentagon. Their business concluded, Alexander walked Griffith to the outer office, shook hands, and went back inside. Everything went downhill from there.

Bristow escorted General Griffith to the Checkmate area, where he talked with quite a few people, including most of the TAC guys who had flown in earlier. They covered lots of territory that day and ended up in a meeting with General Meier in the JCS area, where Griffith, much to his dislike, had to sit through Meier's rendition of the Instant Thunder briefing. This time, Griffith maintained his composure and endured Meier's long-winded explanation of what he wanted to do with the plan. When Meier finished, Griffith excused himself and walked down the second-floor A Ring with Bristow to his waiting chopper. On the way, he told the colonel that he wanted all the TAC guys to back out of whatever they were doing and come home as soon as possible.[12] That was that.

Later on in the week, before Dick Bigelow returned to Langley, leaving only Bristow as guardian of TAC's interests, Bristow called generals Ryan and Griffith, asking for additional TAC people to support the Instant Thunder effort. He argued that Warden and the other planners were actually beginning to make good use of TAC's inputs. If TAC stayed—or, hopefully, increased the number of people on the project—its influence on Instant Thunder could grow substantially. To Bristow's chagrin, the generals denied his request.[13] TAC was leaving the fight.

In the time he had left, Bristow did what he could to help the two Ninth Air Force men. The three of them copied everything they could get their hands on that had anything to do with the Instant Thunder plan. When one of the two Ninth Air Force officers left for Saudi Arabia, he took along the entire plan and most of the supporting documents. His partner, who had left for the theater a few days earlier, also had a suitcase jammed full of Instant Thunder documents, thanks to Bristow's efforts.

The real icing on the cake came in the form of a last-minute message that General Russ wanted Bristow to deliver personally to Meier, the JCS general in charge of the Instant Thunder mess. There was some hope at Langley that this TAC silver bullet, fashioned by Russ himself, might finally kill the beast. Now all Bristow had to do was deliver it.[14]

A bright light suddenly flashed in the colonel's eyes. He shook himself awake, looked around, and saw that they were at the main entrance to Andrews. A security policeman, flashlight in hand, asked for identification. While Bristow dug through his wallet, the young cop kept a careful watch on both men. Security had been tightened ever since the invasion of Kuwait. People were nervous. Rumors about terrorists were already circulating in the Washington area. Bristow handed the airman his green ID card and waited while the policeman compared the picture to Bristow's sleepy face. Bristow had to admit that the photo didn't look much like the tired bird colonel who sat in the passenger seat of this grungy rental car. But it must have been close enough to satisfy the young cop because he returned their cards, stepped back, saluted, and waved them through. Only after the car cleared the guard shack did Bristow see the other security guard, automatic weapon at the ready, standing out of sight near the line of trees.

When the car finally pulled up in front of the passenger service terminal, Bristow was surprised to see so many familiar faces. From the looks of it, Warden must have invited half the guys who were working in Checkmate! Bristow knew that wouldn't go over well with General Meier, who had admonished Warden just the night before to keep the number of people to a minimum.[15] Typically, Warden did just the opposite!

At 0655 the half-full Boeing 727 lifted off and headed south for MacDill AFB. Warden and Meier sat up front in large, first-class seats and quietly went over the briefing, with

Warden pointing out last-minute changes on the slides. Little evidence remained of the acrimonious debate that, at times during the last several days, had periodically flared into shouting matches between the two men and threatened to disrupt the whole effort. Not at all certain that the briefing was of sufficient detail and breadth to satisfy Schwarzkopf, Meier had kept asking that more particulars be added in an attempt to "peel the onion." Warden resisted the changes, arguing that the briefing was exactly what the CINC had called for. The bickering and jabs became so ludicrous that by late evening on 16 August, it wasn't at all clear who would brief General Schwarzkopf the next morning or what exactly they would tell him. Meier even proposed that he and Warden draw straws to determine who would brief the CINC. When that proposal elicited blank, disbelieving stares from Warden and the others, Meier fired back that he would decide on the plane how they would handle it; at the very least, he would make the introductory remarks.[16]

All of this discord took a heavy toll on John Warden. Because work on the Instant Thunder plan consumed his every hour, he had not slept in two days. In fact, the colonel hadn't left the Pentagon until 0500 that morning, when he went home to shower, shave, and put on a fresh uniform before rushing off to catch the plane that would take him to MacDill.[17] Warden was tired—very tired.

Forty-five minutes into the flight, Warden finished his run-through of the briefing slides with General Meier. It had gone well enough, considering. Meier seemed resigned to letting Warden give the overall briefing and having Col Jim Blackburn, the Air Force Intelligence Agency's director of targets, handle the intel portion, as Warden had originally suggested. Meier mollified himself by declaring that he would do the introductions and make comments "worthy of a two-star."[18]

As Warden turned in his seat and bent down to pick up his briefcase, he found himself staring at a pair of feet and ankles. Raising his head, Warden saw that they belonged to Col Dick Bristow. He had no idea how long Bristow had been standing there. The TAC colonel was nervous. His blue collar was rumpled, and a thin line of perspiration had begun to show around his left armpit. His eyes darted back and forth between Warden and General Meier, as if he were having a hard time deciding which man to speak to first. He chose Warden. Bristow stammered out that he needed to talk with General Meier in private and would appreciate it if Warden would leave. Unsure about what Bristow was up to but too tired to care, Warden slowly stood up and then moved to the back of the plane, looking for a place to catch a little sleep before they landed.

Bristow watched Warden walk away and then turned and slid into the colonel's vacant seat. He got right to the point. "I have been asked to give you a message from General Russ." Bristow then told Meier of Russ's grave concerns about the fact that Instant Thunder went from peace to all-out war with no intervening steps. In Russ's view, this massive, *preemptive attack* to win a war against Iraq was very dangerous and could set off a chain reaction that could quickly engulf the world in serious regional conflicts or perhaps even global war. It was dangerous, that's all, and he wanted to make sure that the JCS, the president, and Colin Powell knew it.[19] Meier said nothing. He pursed his lips, frowned, and then bent down to pick up a pen that had fallen to the floor. Finally, he turned to Bristow and told the colonel that he understood Russ's concerns. However, General Powell and the president wanted a plan that would win the war, and they felt that Instant Thunder was the best option to guarantee success. Neither Powell nor the president believed that taking small steps or merely demonstrating our resolve was the way to go. They wanted to win—and win big.[20]

Meier let the weight of his words sink in before turning his gaze back to the window and the clouds below. Bristow—who up to this time had been sitting on the edge of his seat, square-jawed and determined—suddenly went slack. He folded his hands, leaned forward, and rested his elbows on his outstretched knees. Bowing his head, he stared at the cabin floor, not moving a muscle. After a moment, Bristow excused himself and made his way back to the rear of the plane. He spotted Warden curled up in a fetal position, fast asleep on an otherwise empty row of seats along the far right side. Bristow settled back into his own narrow chair, painfully aware that TAC's silver bullet was a dud.

0900/Fri/17 Aug 90/MacDill AFB FL

After getting off the plane, Colonel Warden, General Meier, and the 32 other members of the group took a quick bus ride to General Schwarzkopf's headquarters. It soon became obvious that this briefing would not be a repeat of the low-key, intimate presentation that Warden had made to the CINC the week before in General Moore's office. Warden and his people had top billing now, and it looked like most of the folks at Headquarters CENTCOM had tickets to see the show. In fact, by the time Warden and Meier walked into the CINC's conference room, it was standing room only.[21] Due to what CENTCOM officials said was a problem with transferring security clearances, however, many people who had flown down with Warden were denied entry to the briefing, including a very disappointed Colonel Bristow.*

General Meier made a few opening remarks and turned the briefing over to Colonel Warden, who—despite the dark circles under his eyes—seemed energized and full of enthusiasm. The first portion of the briefing was conceptual in nature and similar to what Warden had briefed the CINC on the week before. When the colonel mentioned keeping casualties to a minimum as one of the campaign's primary objectives, Schwarzkopf interrupted him, a frown beginning to form on his face. "We must make folks understand that there will be civilian casualties."[22]

"Yes," said Warden. Nodding confidently, he explained that a portion of the plan included intensive efforts to show the Iraqis and the world that the responsibility for civilian casualties rested squarely on Saddam Hussein's shoulders and that the coalition would have no choice in the matter.[23] Mollified, Schwarzkopf let the briefing continue. Warden showed the CINC the essential target sets and explained, in general terms, Instant Thunder's emphasis on national paralysis and shock.

Warden turned the Vu-Graph machine off, paused for a moment, and then introduced Jim Blackburn as the intelligence officer charged with giving the CINC a detailed look

---

*Bristow spent most of the briefing in the CENTCOM snack bar and was finally admitted to the briefing area just as Schwarzkopf was leaving. Bristow, 61–62 (see note 3).

at target analysis for Instant Thunder. Blackburn brought out a large map of Iraq that showed target distribution for the air campaign. In quick succession, he highlighted the target complexes around Baghdad and the kinds of weapons they intended to put against them. Included in the target grouping were Baghdad air defenses, command centers, and the presidential palace. Schwarzkopf wanted to know the location of the palace relative to Baghdad.

"Fifteen miles west of Baghdad," said Blackburn, his hand shaking nervously as he pointed to a spot on the large, gray map. Questions from Schwarzkopf weren't making his time in the spotlight any easier. He glanced up at the CINC and pressed on.

Blackburn showed a photo of the Ajaji thermal power plant and explained how strikes from B-52s and TLAMs would take out the switching grid, eliminating 13 percent of Iraq's entire electrical power production and a whopping 60 percent of Baghdad's electrical generation capability. Schwarzkopf seemed pleased with that. Next, Blackburn talked about shutting down the cracking towers at the Al Basrah and Az Yubayr petroleum refineries. By doing so, the intelligence colonel reminded General Schwarzkopf, the air campaign would reduce or stop the flow of oil internally in Iraq yet allow quick recovery of the industry at the war's end, thereby causing little or no harm to Iraq's export capability. Blackburn covered the remainder of the 84 targets in quick succession, with few interruptions from the CINC. Schwarzkopf did express concern with imagery support, but the colonel told him that the Navy and other folks were working the issue. Relieved to have gotten through his portion of the briefing unscathed, Blackburn turned it back over to John Warden and sat down.[24]

Warden, still upbeat and confident, began talking about the execution plan and the weapons systems that would make it happen. When the slide popped up showing the 32 fighter and attack squadrons needed for Instant Thunder execution, the CINC got excited. He pressed Warden about when he thought these forces could be in place and usable. People shifted in their seats, leaned forward, and watched for any sign that the CINC was about to lose his temper. This could get ugly, just as it had on other occasions with different briefers. Most of the staffers in the room were glad that they weren't in Warden's shoes—at least not now.

"We show this by the end of September," said Warden, pointing to the 32 fighter and attack squadrons on the chart. Before anyone could object, he added, "with no prioritization."[25] The CINC nodded and looked at his logistics and operations generals, neither of whom protested. The tension in the room visibly lessened.

When Warden got to the part of the briefing on air superiority, he said apologetically, "Maybe this is more detail than you want." But Schwarzkopf shook his head; he wanted to hear all about it. Warden explained that he really had two concepts of operation in mind here. The first option was to maintain combat air patrols (CAP) with F-15 air superiority fighters south of Baghdad, moving north only if the Iraqis took to the air. The second was to go on a prestrike offensive fighter sweep, destroying Iraqi aircraft on the ground and in the air. In Warden's opinion, this approach would drive Saddam's air forces to autonomous operations by the first morning of the war.[26]

By now it was obvious to almost everyone in the room that the CINC was beginning to like what he was hearing. Warden continued, covering suppression of enemy air defenses and psychological operations. Gathering momentum, he then talked about exactly what the Instant Thunder plan would produce. In Warden's view, the executed plan would destroy Saddam Hussein's power base and leave his offensive military capability degraded and difficult to rebuild. It would also severely disrupt Iraq's economy. Unlike the postwar military, however, Iraq's economy could be quickly restored. Warden referred to this entire effort as a kind of modern-day Schlieffen Plan.*

---

*A war plan conceived in 1906 by Count Alfred von Schlieffen, the German chief of staff, to destroy France before the Russians had time to complete their mobilization. In order to avoid a war on two fronts, Schlieffen wanted to invade France through Belgium with a massive, right-flanking movement. He intended to crush the French forces against their own defenses in an encirclement as effective as the one Hannibal used against the Romans at Cannae, Italy. The German forces would then quickly turn and defeat the Russians. Unfortunately for the Germans, Schlieffen died in 1914, and the execution of the plan fell to Helmuth von Moltke (the younger), who diluted the right flank to support forces engaged against the Russians. Critically weakened, the German offensive stalled and then collapsed. No doubt, General Schwarzkopf was unhappy about Warden's comparing Instant Thunder to a plan that failed.

"Don't call it the Schlieffen Plan!" said Schwarzkopf, gesturing toward the Instant Thunder slides.

"But it *is* the Schlieffen Plan," countered Warden, "rotated into the third dimension!"[27] Since Schwarzkopf did not pursue the argument, the discussion returned to the question of exactly when the forces could be in-theater and available for tasking.

"If we're talking about the end of September, I'm not worried," said Schwarzkopf.

General Meier, who had said nothing since introducing the briefing, piped in, "[Air Force Chief of Staff] Dugan thinks it's executable mid-September and risk-acceptable to do it even earlier."[28]

Schwarzkopf nodded. "We can't flow air and land simultaneously."

"We're not recommending how you make your [flow] choices," said Meier, casting a knowing glance at Warden. The two men had been at odds over making flow recommendations to the CINC ever since Meier got involved in the planning process. Warden wanted to change the flow to get more of the right kinds of aircraft needed to execute Instant Thunder as soon as possible, but Meier was dead-set against even trying to deal with the issue.[29]

Burt Moore, Schwarzkopf's operations general, gestured toward the slides. "These are only forces *assigned* to you. Turkey forces [sic] are not considered, [and] a fourth carrier's not included."[30]

Not wanting to be left out, Warden interjected that during the meeting of 11 August, General Powell indicated that getting permission to use Turkey as a base of operations would be politically difficult.[31] Schwarzkopf cut him off with a wave of the hand, pointed a meaty index finger at him, and said, "I told you to look at a plan not able to launch from Saudi Arabia."[32] The room suddenly went quiet. Now it was Warden's turn to sweat. During the first briefing, the CINC *had* told him to consider an option that didn't include basing in Saudi Arabia. But with only seven days to prepare a comprehensive, executable plan, he simply hadn't had time to think about it, let alone produce something! Besides, in Warden's view, it didn't make any sense! Why plan to commit forces to restore order and economic stability to a region if the major friendly force in that region was unwilling to let you in?

As all of these thoughts converged in Warden's mind, a cold, sickly sensation worked its way from his stomach to his spine. He started to speak but realized the general was still talking. ". . . but the attitude of Arabs today is, Hussein must be rolled back to destroy Iraq as a military power. If we came in and said we could do it in six days, they'd probably wail but would say, 'Don't tell us anything else'." The CINC stood up, tugged at his pants, and broke into a wide smile. "Two-minute break," he barked, heading for the door and a nearby rest room, adding, "You've got me so excited with this!"[33] Warden could hardly believe his ears! A second ago, he thought Schwarzkopf was going to berate him for failing to address the "no-Saudi option." Like Warden, the CINC had evidently concluded that such an option was unnecessary. The queasy feeling left Warden's stomach as quickly as it had appeared.

When Schwarzkopf returned, the large crowd of people who had been milling around, excitedly discussing what they had just seen and heard, fell silent and quickly returned to their seats. Projecting a slide that showed areas of concern, Warden talked about munitions distribution, tanker availability, and the need for a very simple, straightforward airspace control plan.* He also pointed out that long-range, surface-to-surface missiles such as Scuds were going to be an extremely difficult targeting problem. "I won't go into detail," said Warden almost apologetically, as he reached for the pointer and walked to the map, "[but you] don't want them to hit Tel Aviv [and, to a] lesser extent, Riyadh."

Schwarzkopf, feigning surprise, retorted, "*I'll* be in Riyadh! Change the priorities!" The entire room broke into uproarious laughter, except for Warden, who, after a bewildered smile flitted across his lips, continued speaking.

"Extraordinarily difficult problem," he muttered, "AC-130 is a possibility." Because the laughter prompted by the CINC's remark had not yet faded away, most of the people in the room

---

*Airspace control was particularly nettlesome in the Gulf due to varying levels of sophistication in aircraft interrogation systems, language barriers, and the sheer number of aircraft involved.

did not hear Warden's ruminations about using AC-130 gunships as Scud killers.[34]

Before long, the subject turned to doctrine. Warden told the CINC that the Instant Thunder planning had engendered "extraordinary joint integration and cooperation." As far as he could see, there had been "no doctrinal disconnects" between any of the services in the making of the plan. That said, Warden reached into a plain cardboard box and began handing out copies of *The Air Campaign: Planning for Combat*, the book he had written as a student at National Defense University in 1988. He handed one to Schwarzkopf, commenting that he could use the book or simply throw it away. The CINC opened it, looked at a few pages, and then quietly set it aside.[35]

"What's the cost in human life to us?" asked Schwarzkopf.

Warden hesitated a moment. "In my professional judgement," he answered, looking directly at the CINC, "we'll lose 10 to 20 aircraft the first night. After that, less. Three to five percent total."

General Rogers, USCENTCOM vice-commander, emphatically shook his head and frowned. "[I] disagree. I think it will be higher—10 to 15 percent—but we can live with it for a short period."[36]

A murmur washed through the crowd as the significance of what both men were saying sunk in. Most of the audience tended to favor General Rogers's estimate over Warden's. From the looks of things, Iraqi air defenses were going to be tough—real tough. In fact, some of the aviators in the room were convinced that the loss rates would be much higher than either man predicted.

Warden waited until the noise abated and then calmly walked over to General Rogers. "I'll tell you why I think losses will be lower," said Warden in a kindly, professorial tone. He carefully explained how Instant Thunder's massive attacks on the Iraqi air defense system in the first 15 minutes of the war would simply overwhelm it, causing confusion and paralysis. According to Warden, the Iraqi air defenses were actually not all that good and certainly could be suppressed. After the first day or two of the war, Warden argued, coalition forces would have almost complete air superiority throughout the operating area. "I'm a volunteer to fly," said Warden, smiling broadly.[37]

Rogers, his arms folded in front of him, was still unimpressed. "You've answered most [of my questions]," he said glumly, "but you've ignored Kuwait.[38] I don't think we can flank Kuwait."[39]

"I'm not worried about ground forces in Kuwait,"[40] said Schwarzkopf impatiently, as he massaged his jaw with his left hand. "Can you fly around ground-to-air defenses building [up] in Kuwait?"

Warden started to reply, but General Moore beat him to it. "[We] can do lethal or nonlethal suppression."

"We can even do *deception* to induce them to put SAMs [surface-to-air missiles] in Kuwait," said Warden, a glint in his eye. "[It's] a good place for them!"[41]

Schwarzkopf smiled at the comment and nodded his head in approval. The briefing turned back to logistics and basing, with the principals voicing concern over the possibility of quickly saturating the operating bases in Saudi and elsewhere.

"How long to build up an infrastructure [to handle the flow of forces and materiel]?" asked Schwarzkopf.

"[We're] not sure [that] in a week and a half we've answered *all* the questions," replied Meier cautiously. The JCS two-star did not want the CINC to believe that this little group he had brought down from Washington knew everything. A lot more work needed to be done.[42]

Bob Johnston, Schwarzkopf's chief of staff—a ramrod-straight, perfectly chiseled Marine two-star—volunteered his thoughts on the subject. "[We] might want to *protract*, to build SEAD capability. Do we have a plan to stretch this out logistically?"[43]

The CINC shot Johnston a disgusted look, growling, "By the end of the first week we'll have all kinds of pressure to get out![44] The [United Nations] Security Council will scream. If we can be done in six days, we can say we're sorry and get out. [It] may not be pretty, but we're gonna get this."[45]

General Meier, realizing that Schwarzkopf was leaning heavily in favor of Instant Thunder, jumped in and summarized the plan's advantages one more time.[46] His words whipped Schwarzkopf into a frenzy.

"This is what makes the US a superpower!" shouted the CINC as he pointed to the Instant Thunder slides. "This uses our strengths against their weaknesses, not our small army against their large army." He half stood up and slammed his open palm down hard on the tabletop, his eyes glistening and his jaw jutting forward. "Our *air power* against theirs is [the] way to go—that's why I called you guys in the first place!"[47]

"What can we do for you?" asked Meier, his eyes moving from Schwarzkopf to Warden and the assembled Washington team and back again to Schwarzkopf.[48]

"[The] first assistance is him," said Schwarzkopf, pointing a finger at Warden. The CINC turned, faced the colonel, and stared. It was curious to watch Schwarzkopf, a burly hulk of a man, his face huge and fleshy, peering down at the smaller, angular John Warden—rather like a bear taking the measure of a wolf. "Go to Riyadh with at least one other," ordered Schwarzkopf. "I'm sending you to Riyadh, to Horner—to brief him," he said again, still staring. "To hand [the] plan off. My intention is to continue to plan, to *refine* it to [the] point of execution."[49]

Schwarzkopf relaxed a little and walked over to Warden. "Don't *leave* the package,"* he cautioned. "Carry and *deliver* it to Chuck Horner." The CINC looked at General Meier. "Any problem?"

"No problem, sir," Meier replied. "How soon?"

"We're at war," snorted the CINC. "The sooner, the better."[50]

Notes

1. Air Staff Protocol Document: President Bush/SECDEF Meeting, 13 August 1990, Deptula file 5, Desert Story Collection, US Air Force Historical Research Agency, Maxwell AFB, Ala.

---

*Hours before the briefing, General Schwarzkopf received a call from General Dugan, who told him that if he liked the plan and wanted to implement it, he should consider it his own and make certain his air component commander, General Horner, understood that. Unless Schwarzkopf owned the plan, it might encounter opposition (e.g., from Horner) and prove unworkable. Gen Michael J. Dugan, Washington, D.C., transcript of interview with author, 15 August 1991, 13–14, Desert Story Collection, US Air Force Historical Research Agency, Maxwell AFB, Ala.

2. David Hoffman and Patrick E. Tyler, "Bush Denounces Saddam as Threat to Arabs, West," *Washington Post,* 16 August 1990, A31.

3. Col Richard D. Bristow, Langley AFB, Va., transcript of interview with Lt Col Edward C. Mann and author, 9 November 1992, 43–44, Desert Story Collection, US Air Force Historical Research Agency, Maxwell AFB, Ala.

4. Ibid., 32.

5. Ibid., 38–39.

6. Ibid., 38.

7. Ibid.

8. Lt Gen Robert M. Alexander, Washington, D.C., transcript of interview with Lt Col Suzanne B. Gehri, Lt Col Edward C. Mann, and author, 3 June 1992, 20, Desert Story Collection, US Air Force Historical Research Agency, Maxwell AFB, Ala.

9. Ibid., 21.

10. Ibid.

11. Ibid.

12. Bristow, 9 November 1992, 43.

13. Ibid., 43, 46–48.

14. Ibid., 15, 58.

15. Lt Col Dave Deptula and Maj Buck Rogers, Maxwell AFB, Ala., transcript of interview with Lt Col Suzanne B. Gehri, Lt Col Edward C. Mann, and author, 22 May 1991, 20, Desert Story Collection, US Air Force Historical Research Agency, Maxwell AFB, Ala.

16. Notes, Lt Col Ben Harvey, 77–86, Desert Story Collection, US Air Force Historical Research Agency, Maxwell AFB, Ala. (Secret) Information extracted here and in subsequent references is unclassified. Hereinafter referred to as Harvey. See also Deptula and Rogers, 22 May 1991, 4–20, for an expanded account of the difficulties between Warden and Meier.

17. Bristow, 9 November 1992, 56.

18. Deptula and Rogers, 22 May 1991, 15.

19. Bristow, 9 November 1992, 15, 58. For a more detailed look at General Russ's view, see Gen Robert D. Russ, Alexandria, Va., transcript of interview with Lt Col Suzanne B. Gehri, Lt Col Edward C. Mann, and author, 9 December 1991, 8–14, Desert Story Collection, US Air Force Historical Research Agency, Maxwell AFB, Ala.

20. Bristow, 9 November 1992, 15.

21. Harvey, 88.

22. Personal notes, Lt Col Dave Deptula. Information extracted here and in subsequent references is unclassified. Hereinafter referred to as Deptula.

23. Harvey, 88.

24. Ibid., 89, 90.

25. Ibid., 90.

26. Ibid., 91.

27. Ibid., 92.

28. Ibid.

29. Ibid., 71–93.

30. Ibid., 93.

31. Col John A. Warden III, Washington, D.C., transcript of interview with Lt Col Suzanne B. Gehri, Lt Col Edward C. Mann, and author, 30 May

1991, 120–21, Desert Story Collection, US Air Force Historical Research Agency, Maxwell AFB, Ala.

32. Harvey, 93.
33. Ibid.
34. Ibid., 94–95.
35. Ibid., 95.
36. Ibid.; and Deptula.
37. Harvey, 96.
38. Ibid.
39. Deptula.
40. Ibid.
41. Harvey, 96.
42. Ibid., 97.
43. Ibid., 97–98.
44. Deptula.
45. Harvey, 98.
46. Ibid.
47. Ibid.; and Deptula.
48. Harvey, 98.
49. Ibid., 98–99.
50. Ibid., 99.

Chapter 7

1740/Sat/18 Aug 90/Andrews AFB MD

The heat was unbearable. Sweat ran in rivulets down Lt Col Dave Deptula's face as he struggled to find a comfortable spot in the rear of the overcrowded aircraft. The big, four-engined RC-135 had been waiting on the ramp at Andrews for almost an hour now, delayed by thunderstorms that were rumbling up and down the East Coast. At first, Deptula tried to read *The Role of Airpower in the Iran-Iraq War*,[1] a thin paperback he had stuffed into his briefcase at the last moment, but the stifling heat and close quarters made concentration difficult.

Col John Warden was nearby, amid a jumble of boxes and cargo gear, wearing the same flight suit he had worn as commander of the 36th Tactical Fighter Wing in Bitburg, Germany, several years ago.* His flying attire was a bit unusual and stood out, even to the most casual military observer. Whereas "bags"** usually had a single unit-identifier patch on the upper right shoulder, Warden's was replete with the three fighter squadron patches from his old Bitburg wing. A colorful menagerie of bulldogs, bumblebees, and tigers ran from his shoulder to his elbow.

Despite the heat and cramped conditions, Warden appeared happier and more relaxed than anyone had seen him in a long time. The third member of Warden's group, Lt Col Ben Harvey, a small, dark-haired man in his early forties, was sitting quietly and making entries in what appeared to be a diary. To his left was the last member of the group, Lt Col Ron Stanfill, a big-boned, brusque, F-111 pilot who almost didn't get to make the trip. Warden had wanted Stanfill to stay at the Pentagon and mind the store while he, Deptula, and Harvey went to Riyadh. But Stanfill had pleaded with Warden, citing his abilities as a weaponeer and planner, arguing with the colonel that his presence was absolutely necessary. At first, Warden refused, saying that too many people would be going into

---

*Warden commanded this unit from August 1987 to January 1988.
**Aircrew slang for flight suit.

113

theater. Before long, however, under increasing pressure from Stanfill, Warden relented and allowed him to go.[2]

None of that mattered now. Warden and the others could hear the big engines change pitch from a rumble to a roar as the heavily loaded reconnaissance plane charged down the runway and clawed its way into an angry Maryland sky. Deptula pressed his head back against the bulkhead, grateful for the first rush of cool air that poured into the cargo area from the now-operating air-conditioning system. Thank God he'd had enough sense to borrow a few larger, more comfortable flight suits from his good friend Maj Buck Rogers! He closed his eyes and smiled, remembering how his wife, Dianna, although protesting loudly, managed to get his rank sewn on and everything packed before he made his hasty departure.[3]

His reverie was interrupted when Colonel Warden tapped him gently on the shoulder and told him that he wanted to go over the briefing material several more times during the trip, just in case they had missed an item or needed to add something to the attack plan. As it stood, Instant Thunder was jammed into two four-inch-thick black binders, the product of thousands of man-hours of intensive, meticulous effort.

The document they would present to Horner was no simple target list but a comprehensive, theater-level operations plan. It included targets, attack routes, timing, special operations, strategies, deceptions, commander's intents—the whole nine yards. Nevertheless, Warden told Deptula and the others that they couldn't afford to be too confident. The fact that they had won the battle of Washington didn't mean that the battle for the hearts and minds of CENTAF, especially General Horner's, was going to be a cakewalk.[4]

1730/Sun/19 Aug 90/Riyadh, Saudi Arabia

The late afternoon sun hovered low over the Saudi desert as Warden's jet touched down in Riyadh and taxied to a halt, 20 hours after leaving Andrews. Except for a brief stop at Hellenikon AB, outside of Athens, Greece, they had been in the air the entire time. To Deptula, the environment reminded him

114

of his days in Phoenix, Arizona, when he went through F-15 upgrade training. It was blast-furnace hot, and dry as bone. The travelers dragged their bags through the heat and waited for a ride to Royal Saudi Air Force headquarters. Before long, a car pulled up, driven by an Air Force lieutenant colonel named Lauberbach.[5]

Lauberbach was agitated because he was expecting only one person. His tiny car—jammed with chemical protection gear, bottled water, and an odd assortment of cups and glasses—couldn't possibly hold all five of them! Deptula, Harvey, and Stanfill agreed that Warden would accompany the lieutenant colonel to headquarters and that another driver would come back later to pick them up. But the sun had long set before they were finally reunited with Colonel Warden at RSAF headquarters. Without the briefing materials, the colonel had been able to do little in their absence but wander the halls and make discreet inquiries about when his companions would arrive from the airfield.

The four planners ate a quick dinner and discussed what would come next. CENTAF staffers had gotten word that Warden had been scheduled to brief them at 1600. When he didn't show up, they assumed the briefing had been cancelled. Warden told Deptula and the others that the briefing was rescheduled for 2200 that evening. Only key members of the CENTAF staff would be there. They would have to deal with Horner later.

2200/Sun/19 Aug 90/HQ RSAF/ Riyadh, Saudi Arabia

Warden and his party gathered in the narrow, spit-and-polish conference room on the third floor of RSAF head-quarters at the appointed hour but had to cool their heels for almost 30 minutes while they waited for General Olsen, Horner's deputy. Waiting with them were Brig Gen Pat Caruana, Horner's strategic forces advisor; Brig Gen Larry Henry, an electronic warfare expert; Col Jim Crigger, CENTAF director of operations; Col John Leonardo, CENTAF director of intelligence; and Lt Col Sam Baptiste, Ninth Air Force weapons and tactics expert, who had accompanied Lt Col Foose Wilson to his meeting with General Horner the week before. Wilson was there too, looking tired and frustrated. He elbowed Deptula and whispered that he would talk to him later about what had been going on.[6]

When General Olsen finally arrived, the briefing quickly got under way. As Warden worked through the slides, the CENTAF staffers seemed very interested and attentive. They asked some questions about aircraft selection for targets in downtown Baghdad, and then General Olsen and Ron Stanfill spent considerable time agreeing that F-111Fs were infinitely preferable to the F-111Ds currently scheduled to come into theater. Near the end of the briefing, Olsen smiled broadly and told the group that the Instant Thunder plan "sounded like a good start" and that he hoped they had "brought more than three days of clothes."[7] According to Olsen, the Instant Thunder plan was exactly what they had wanted to build, but they had simply run out of time and focused on the near term.[8]

Jim Crigger gave the Checkmate group a thumbnail sketch of the D day plan that his staff and almost everyone else in CENTAF had been working on since their arrival in-theater. This all-out defensive plan to blunt an attack on Saudi Arabia and her oil fields was the near-term effort Olsen had alluded to earlier.* A lot of people in Riyadh were convinced that the heavily armored Iraqi ground forces that rolled through Kuwait were getting ready to launch an attack into Saudi Arabia as well. Horner was one of them.[9]

"Right now," said General Olsen as he paused and took a long drink from his water glass, "we're fully employed just trying to pull things together. In a week we'll have more people. I'd have to pull people out of jobs," he said, nodding toward the intelligence and operations directors, "[in order] to assign [them] to [a] special study group [i.e., Instant Thunder planning]. I *could* do it," he said slowly, biting his lower lip and wrinkling his forehead.[10]

---

*By mid-September 1990, Horner had de-emphasized the plan when it became apparent that the Iraqis were moving to a defensive posture in Kuwait.

During the awkward pause, Olsen possibly was remembering how quickly the Iraqis had roared through Kuwait and was weighing what kind of effort he could afford to divert from the D day plan to Instant Thunder. Before the invasion, intelligence sources had assured them that Iraqi forces would need about a month to take Kuwait. Instead, the Iraqis were able to park their tanks at the Saudi border only three days after the invasion started! The Instant Thunder plan seemed to offer a fundamentally sound way of countering the Iraqi threat with air power alone, and—as Olsen had to admit—the only thing CENTCOM had in-theater these days was air power.[11]

"People need to work this *and* [the] defensive campaign,"[12] said Crigger.

Everyone at the meeting seemed to agree that Instant Thunder was a welcome addition to CENTAF's planning arsenal. Larry Henry, the only person who had any serious problems with the plan, wasn't even a bona fide member of the CENTAF staff. A lanky, leather-faced brigadier general, Henry was known for his heroic exploits as an F-4 backseater in the Vietnam War. He had been sent into theater only days before by Gen Bob Russ, the TAC commander, to assist Horner with electronic warfare planning. Like so many others who followed in the months ahead, Henry—at this time—had no official title or position in the CENTAF hierarchy—he was simply there to help.

Henry objected to what appeared to him to be an assignment of forces by route packs*—a throwback to the Vietnam era. He argued that this kind of targeting would cause doctrinal problems among the services. Dave Deptula, who had put together the attack portions of Instant Thunder, assured the general that they had no intention of fragmenting the attack plan into segments controlled by each service (i.e., Navy, Marine Corps, and Air Force).

---

*A targeting procedure used during the Vietnam War, whereby each service operated in a particular attack area (i.e., a route pack) and assumed responsibility for its own separation and safety. This system eliminated the need for one service to coordinate closely with the other services while it operated in the attack area but prevented the optimization of weapons and aircraft against enemy targets. The term *packs* is the GI shortening of the word *packages*, which refers to the multiple aircraft packages that flew the various routes within the theater.

He explained that, because of the long distances to many of the targets, the planners assigned targets based on the proximity of friendly forces. Thus, the Marine Corps and the Persian Gulf battle group would strike targets in southeastern Iraq and Kuwait; the Air Force would take the center section of Iraq and some of the western approaches; and the Red Sea task force would focus primarily on the western portion of Iraq.[13] But none of this would preclude the use of appropriate weapons and aircraft across the entire breadth of Iraq and Kuwait. The explanation apparently satisfied Henry since he let the issue drop, and they quickly moved on to other things.

The meeting didn't adjourn until well after midnight. By that time, Warden and his colleagues had been up for over 24 hours and needed some sleep. They were given the keys to a small car and told to find their way to the White Palace Hotel, where reservations had been made for them. The four men drove around for almost an hour, the gas gauge of the white sedan edging down and then settling firmly on empty, before one of them spotted the place. When they tried to check in, the clerk told them—to their dismay—that the hotel had given away their rooms! Deptula sat dejectedly on a jumble of suitcases at curbside, halfheartedly scribbling notes, while Warden and Stanfill persuaded the reluctant clerk to let them sleep on cots in the ballroom rather than send them out into the night.[14]

Before long, the four planners joined about 300 other hapless souls in the hotel ballroom, where they quickly undressed and slid into bed. As the others drifted off to sleep, Warden lay awake, staring at the huge filigreed ceiling. He could hardly contain himself. The plan—*his* plan—was really coming together. They had been in Riyadh less than six hours, but the CENTAF vice-commander and other important members of Horner's staff already had given them thumbs-up on Instant Thunder! Before leaving the headquarters building, Olsen had told the colonel and his party that they should come back in the morning so he could take them around and help them get oriented.[15] With any luck, mused Warden, as he rolled over and pulled the single white sheet up around his shoulders, he and the rest of his team would be asked to stay and "pick up the responsibility for doing the strategic planning for General Horner."[16] With that tantalizing thought racing around his head, John Warden fell into a fitful sleep.

0630/Mon/20 Aug 90/Riyadh, Saudi Arabia

Warden arose the next morning and trundled down to the indoor swimming pool area along with Deptula, Harvey, and Stanfill for a hot shower and a shave. When they returned to the hotel cafe, they were pleasantly surprised to find a first-rate breakfast buffet. The sight of the delicately arranged fruits, juices, and cereals and the aroma of freshly brewed Arabian coffee made them realize how long it had been since they had anything decent in their stomachs. For the first time since they had been on the trip, there was little conversation between them as they piled their plates high with delicacies and made their way back to the table. They ate ravenously, thinking about what the day would bring. In less than an hour, they were ready to go.

General Olsen proved true to his word. After they arrived at RSAF headquarters at 0800, they were taken to the basement, where they met a large number of operations and intelligence people and then toured the tactical air control center. Everyone seemed helpful and full of enthusiasm. As Warden and his colleagues walked through the headquarters, people were saying, "How can we help you? What can we do? What do you need?"[17] Good news and pleasant feelings seemed to pile one on top of the other.

Before long, Warden got word that he was scheduled to brief General Horner at 1330. He was ebullient! This was the moment he had been waiting for—the reason he had travelled to Saudi Arabia in the first place. At last he would have a chance to give a face-to-face explanation of Instant Thunder to the man Schwarzkopf had charged with executing it. Perhaps if Warden had listened more closely to Foose Wilson, he would have understood exactly what kind of a minefield he was walking into and wouldn't have been quite so eager to go through it.

Foose had talked candidly to Dave Deptula about all the things he had encountered at CENTAF since his arrival the week before. In Wilson's view, the CENTAF staff had no leadership and was wandering adrift. Although the combat operations staff continued to work on the immediate problem of "what if the Iraqis cross the line with tanks," nobody seemed interested in long-term issues and problems.[18] Wilson complained bitterly to Deptula that CENTAF's total effort was directed at tactical-level details and that no one was looking at employing air power offensively with a strategic plan. He even bridled over the Saudis' stingy allocation of floor space in their Pentagon-sized facility. They'd given CENTAF just two rooms for all their people and equipment. It was preposterous! According to Wilson, ever since he had arrived in Riyadh, everyone had been slow-rolling him.[19] He was afraid that after Deptula and the others left, the plan they had brought with them would die of neglect. The afternoon briefing would prove Wilson wrong. The object was not neglect—but murder.

1355/Mon/20 Aug 90/HQ RSAF/ Riyadh, Saudi Arabia

John Warden rearranged his slides and other briefing paraphernalia for what seemed to be the hundredth time as he waited for General Horner to appear. Foose Wilson's pessimism had done little to dissuade Warden from his firm belief that, given a chance, he could convince the general—or anyone else—of the efficacy of the Instant Thunder plan. Not that Warden believed he was such a great briefer. On the contrary, he hardly gave a thought to his own capabilities. To him, ideas and concepts mattered—not people. If a great plan like Instant Thunder were properly explained, even the harshest, most jaded critic would see its value. All it took was patience and a clear understanding of the subject. The rest would follow. Still, the colonel couldn't help noticing that his fingers were clammy and his mouth seemed uncomfortably dry.

Suddenly, Warden was jolted out of his reverie by the crash of chairs slamming against the heavy wooden table as people struggled to rise from their seats and stand at attention in the 12′ x 35′ briefing room. Horner had arrived. The stocky three-star grunted out a "take your seats" as he ambled to his place, pulled out a chair, and sat down. He didn't look happy. How could he be? Since departing the States on 4 August, he had been working nonstop as the CENTCOM forward commander. His every waking hour had been consumed with coordinating land, sea, and air deployments; working host-nation issues; dealing with the State Department; soothing the media; and a hundred other equally absorbing tasks. He'd been up all hours of the night talking with key decision makers in the United States and Europe, including his own boss, General Schwarzkopf. Horner had precious little time to think about his *real* job as CENTAF commander. However, until the CINC arrived, it looked as though he were going to have to rely on Tom Olsen and the rest of the staff to keep things going in the RSAF compound. For a guy who was used to running his own air show, this had been a tough, very frustrating couple of weeks.

Warden hurried over to the three-star and placed a large bag in front of him. Horner gave the colonel a puzzled look and then gingerly peeked inside.

"What is this [expletive deleted]?" he asked.[20]

Warden hastily explained that the bag contained all the lip balm, razors, and suntan lotion that he, Deptula, and Stanfill could find in the few hours they had before reporting to Andrews AFB for the trip to Riyadh. Their boss, Lt Gen Jimmie Adams, suggested they bring these items because he had heard they were in short supply in-theater and thought the CENTAF people could use them.[21] Horner's face twisted into a sneer as he roughly shoved the heavy package aside. "Proceed,"[22] was all he said.

Not far into the briefing, Horner interrupted Warden in mid-sentence. "Go, go!" he said, grimacing and waving his hands impatiently at the slides. "I know all that!"[23]

Horner's imperiousness seemed to deflate Warden. He seemed nervous and unsteady, no longer the plucky colonel who had put on smooth, forceful performances in front of Schwarzkopf and Powell. The simple fact was that despite his many years in the Air Force fighter community, rudeness or vulgarity made John Warden uncomfortable. He didn't behave that way, and he couldn't understand why others would. It confused him.

Warden took a deep breath and looked at Horner. The general's tired, red-rimmed eyes revealed nothing—or at least nothing Warden could make sense of. It was curious that these two men were so far apart intellectually and emotionally. Both wore flight suits, both were fighter pilots, and both had done combat tours in Vietnam. Unquestionably, their records indicated they were supremely capable airmen. Yet, they seemed to have no common lineage—nothing upon which to build mutual trust or confidence. Thoroughly unsettled, Warden turned back to his slides.

Horner let Warden run through the rest of the briefing with few additional interruptions. As the colonel explained each of the charts and diagrams, Horner sat stonefaced, occasionally mumbling to himself. Although the room was jammed with CENTAF people—Olsen, Crigger, Henry, and everyone else present at last night's briefing—all of them were strangely silent.

When Warden concluded, Horner coughed and remarked that he had a "little trouble" with the plan's basic premise of severing Iraq's head from its body. "This may work in the short term, but [in] 20 years [it] will be disaster. [It will] create hatred against America!"[24]

Horner began to pick at the specifics of the plan, insinuating that it directed too much energy toward the destruction of Iraq's strategic air defense system rather than its neutralization. "Did you do analysis of destruction versus neutralization?"[25] he asked.

Warden did not answer directly. Instead, he talked about Instant Thunder's commitment of 35–40 percent of coalition forces to the destruction of Iraqi aircraft on the ground.[26] It was almost as though the two men were talking to each other on different frequencies. Impatient and visibly frustrated with his inability to get Warden to answer him directly, Horner turned to Colonel Crigger, his operations director.

"Jim, take a look," he said, pointing in the general direction of Warden and his slides. "[It] may be [a] poor way to dedicate effort."[27] Horner then shifted in his seat and leaned forward, staring hard at the thin-lipped colonel from Washington.

"What percentage of the effort is being used to eliminate [Saddam Hussein]?" he asked. "Did you study his command and control?"

"The study's not good," shot back Warden in a tone that surprised even him. He remembered the incomplete and shoddily prepared report on the Iraqi C^2 system he had stumbled across in Washington the week before. It offered little to his planners, and he couldn't imagine it doing anything for the general.

Horner frowned and turned to Colonel Leonardo, his intelligence officer. "John," he said, gravel in his voice, "we must study his C^2. [We] want to make *sure* we destroy his command and control."

"[You] can't make sure," someone commented from the front of the briefing room. All heads turned to see who had spoken. It was Warden.

Horner talked slowly now, his jaw clenched, a hard edge forming on every word. "Not your job. *We'll* make sure. You made an academic study," he said, chewing on the word *academic* as though it were something distasteful. "I've got to make it reality."[28]

For a moment, no one said anything. The muffled sounds of Riyadh street traffic three floors below crept into the room. Sensing that he had somehow offended the general, Warden cleared his throat and stepped back from the table. Horner continued.

"What's the goal of [attacking] the railroads?" he asked. "What's the goal of the airfield attacks?"

Warden began to answer, but Horner—obviously irritated—interrupted him. "What's the goal of the ports disruption? Is this a mulligan stew? I'm not quite sure why you're doing all this," he said, shaking his head and looking up and down the table at his staff. They said nothing. Turning back to Warden, the general asked, "Do you know what the [Iraqi military] storage and production usage rates are?"[29] Before Warden could answer, Horner pointed a finger at Colonel Leonardo and said, "John, look at storage versus production."[30]

Only when Horner asked a question about the use of Navy TLAMs was Warden able to reestablish a dialogue with him.

Horner was concerned that using TLAMs, which had a relatively small warhead (750–1,000 pounds), would be an expensive waste of effort.[31] Warden assured him that the Navy missiles were necessary because they made possible the daylight attack of heavily defended sites in downtown Baghdad without the risk of losing aircrews.[32] Mollified, Horner moved on to the Instant Thunder slide that showed coalition forces in the initial attack packages.

"[That] bullet on multinational forces is interesting," he commented, pointing to the slide.

Warden agreed, saying, "[The] chairman of the Joint Chiefs of Staff wants non-US [forces] to bleed and die [as well]."[33] The colonel then launched into a detailed discussion of the types of forces available to execute the Instant Thunder plan and the strategic and tactical significance of the targets assigned to each force. The longer Warden talked, the more bored Horner became.

"Well look," he said waving his hand in disgust. "Let's not use the terms *strategic* and *tactical*. Targets are targets." Anxious to move Warden on to another subject, he asked, "What does the night buy you?" Before Warden could explain all the nuances of the first night strike, the general interrupted him yet again.

"Let's be honest," he said. "People are going to die! Don't deconflict by route packages. We did that in Vietnam; we'll never do that again."[34] Horner let out a long sigh and shook his head in exasperation. He sucked air in between his clenched teeth and asked Warden, "In your thinking, were you going to overwhelm [the enemy] or apply continuous pressure?"[35]

"Both, really," said Warden.

"I think you'd want to do both," said Horner approvingly. "I *need* to do both! I'm looking at 600 sorties each [day]." Horner pointed at Leonardo and Crigger. "You two take a look at what would be required to conduct an overwhelming strike versus what we need to conduct a sustained campaign."[36]

For the next few minutes, Horner and his staff discussed targeting strategies while Warden and his assistants looked on. It soon became clear that CENTAF's focus was at the tactical—not strategic—level of warfare. Sortie generation, tactics, and load-outs were the topics of the day. The broader question of what they should do with their air power never seemed to occur to them. As the talk continued, Warden's stomach grew tighter, and his face flushed. This was going to be harder than even he had imagined. CENTAF was stuck in the weeds.

The conversation soon turned back to the Instant Thunder plan and the people who brought it.

"[Your] main effort was to do targeting," said Horner. "[We] need to rethink targeting philosophy."[37]

Horner then ordered his staff to remove the deployment and readiness time lines Warden had briefed for the Instant Thunder plan, arguing that they served no purpose other than to advertise a totally unrealistic completion date for a notional war plan. Warden argued with the general, saying that everyone in the chain, including General Schwarzkopf, was driving to a mid-September execution date. Horner didn't seem to care. As the acting CENTCOM forward commander, he was convinced that his command could be ready for combat operations no earlier than the end of September, when the 2d Armored Division would arrive in-theater.[38] Horner made it clear that he would not feel comfortable about CENTCOM's ability to defend Saudi Arabia against attack until a strong US Army contingent showed up. Offensive options could come later.

"We'll take this target list that you've given us," he said, refusing to acknowledge that Instant Thunder was, by all rights, a theater-level operations plan. "We'll refine it, but we'd better be able to defend; we'd better be able to execute; and it['d] better work. . . . How we do it depends on the dispersal of hostages* and how that plays.[39] El Dorado Canyon was probably five times harder!"[40] Apparently, Horner was convinced that the planning required to bring down Iraq would be nowhere near as difficult as the planning involved in the 1986 raid against Muammar Qadhafi's forces in Libya.

"Yes, sir!" chimed in Ronnie Stanfill, grateful for a chance to say something to Horner and the staff. "But [our aircrews] won't have much combat experience."[41] As Stanfill waxed

---

*Americans held by Saddam Hussein in Iraq and Kuwait.

eloquent about his role in the planning for El Dorado Canyon, John Warden was quietly coming apart.

He simply could not believe what he had heard. Could Horner really be so naive as to think that planning the takedown of Iraq would be simpler than the planning required for a one-time raid on Libya? Did the man really not understand what was involved here and what was at stake? Why was he so focused on this defensive nonsense? Didn't he see the danger in that? Warden frantically tried to decide what to do next. Somehow, he had to get Horner thinking strategically! But how?

"[I] think we need to put more on Hussein,"[42] said Warden, in a casual, off-handed way. It appeared that Warden was offering some bait in an attempt to move the general in the right direction.

"[I'm] skeptical about getting Hussein,"[43] said Horner, giving a knowing wink to his intelligence officer.

Warden leaned forward and put his thin, well-manicured hands on the polished conference table. "[It's] not imperative to *get* him," he answered slowly. "[We] need [only] to isolate him for a while."[44]

Horner cupped his face in his hands and rubbed his tired eyes. He had little patience left. This staff puke from Washington with his academic answers was making it hard for him to keep from blowing up.

"Our goal," said Horner, pulling himself up from a slouching position in his chair and glaring at Warden, "[is to] build an A—T—O!"[45] Horner was almost shouting now, his voice squeezing out each word. "[The operation] should be open-ended, *beyond six days;** [the goal], gut Iraq."[46] Horner paused for a moment and rested his meaty forearms on the table, drawing circles on the polished surface with his index finger. Calmer now, he said, "[It isn't] necessarily [a war] against the Iraqi people. [As it is,] we'll incur a 200-year penalty because you're [sic] not Arab." The three-star continued, saying, "[We] must give [the] CINC [this] option in [the] event of unacceptable Iraqi behavior."[47]

---

*Instant Thunder called for a six-to-nine-day execution phase.

Horner looked back again at John Warden. A smile flickered across his lips as the anger ebbed from his eyes. "[I'll] take [your] list and refine [it] a bit," he said, nodding toward the binders containing the Instant Thunder attack plan. "[There are] some good things," he grudgingly acknowledged, "[like] leadership [and] command and control." He paused for a moment. "[But I] don't think we have a good feel for [the] defensive [battle] yet."[48]

Horner then launched into a discussion on the advantages of various weapons platforms, including the B-52. He wanted aircraft and equipment that did not compromise his ability to defend Saudi Arabia from attack.[49]

Something Warden said earlier had been gnawing at Horner all through the meeting. If it were true, the planning for any operation—offensive or defensive—would be much more difficult. Horner had to be certain.

"From [the] chairman of the Joint Chiefs of Staff is [the] assumption [the war plan] *must* be multinational?" he asked skeptically.

"Yes, sir," replied Warden, his heart pounding wildly.

Horner frowned, tapping his forehead. He ordered his staff to "build this in isolation," meaning without multinational planning assistance. "[The] idea is not to hide [the plan] from the Saudis but to build [it] before we explain it to them. I'm still uncomfortable about the target list," he added. "I don't see [Instant Thunder] as a slick plan but as a 'hit-him-in-the-face' [kind of thing]."[50]

"How many times have we done this? Twenty?" he asked his staff, leaning back, his arms outstretched. [expletive deleted], he chortled, "this is not an exercise!"[51] Horner then lamented the fact that it was taking so long for ground forces to get in-theater while he faced a massive Iraqi armored threat only hours from his headquarters.

Warden could stand it no longer. All this talk from Horner about focusing on the defense and about waiting for *land* forces to arrive and now—in his view—a perfectly irrational concern on the general's part about Iraqi armor perched behind sand berms a hundred miles away in the desert made Warden angry. Hadn't Horner heard anything that he had been saying? Instant Thunder obviated the need for all of those concerns.

"You're being overly pessimistic about those tanks,"[52] he said curtly to the three-star. It was classic John Warden. Instantly, a hush fell over the room. At the far end of the table, someone's wristwatch started beeping. In the tense silence, the tiny noise seemed louder than the wails of air-raid sirens being tested around the city. If Warden heard the sound, he didn't show it. Perhaps he didn't care. He rested his hand on the planning binders and went on talking. "Ground forces aren't important to [the] campaign," he said, matter-of-factly, shrugging his shoulders and gesturing toward the general. "I don't believe they can move under [our] air superiority."[53]

During the ensuing silence, Horner stared daggers at the colonel. The muscles in his jaw twitched, but still he said nothing. At first, Warden stared back at the brooding three-star, frustrated that he was unable to make him understand and accept the Instant Thunder plan. After what seemed an eternity, Warden looked around the room and saw that no one else was moving. Even Harvey, Stanfill, and Deptula were staring straight ahead. It was as though everyone, save Horner and Warden, was afraid to take a breath. Warden turned his gaze back to General Horner and looked him in the eyes.

"I apologize,"[54] he said softly.

The three-star swiveled around and, with his back to Warden, said mockingly, "I'm being very, very patient, aren't I?"[55]

"Yes, sir!"[56] said someone in the room.

"I'm being very, very tolerant, aren't I?"[57]

"Yes, sir!"[58] the same person replied, even more loudly. The other staffers began to nod their heads vigorously.

"I'm really being nice not to make the kind of response that you-all would expect me to make, aren't I?"[59]

"Oh, yes, sir!"[60] the same voice agreed. The other staffers all nodded their heads in unison.

Satisfied, Horner turned back to Warden, the smile disappearing from his face. "I accept your apology,"[61] he deadpanned.

A sigh of relief filled the room, and things quickly returned to normal. Well, almost normal. The curious thing was that after the outburst, John Warden, for all practical purposes, ceased to exist—at least in Horner's eyes and those of the CENTAF staff. Despite the fact that he was standing in their midst at the head of the briefing table, Horner no longer addressed him; consequently, neither did anyone else on the CENTAF staff. After a while, numb with disbelief and utter despair at what he perceived as the failure of his mission, Warden shuffled over to a nearby chair and sank down.

Horner, on the other hand, seemed energized and happy after the exchange. He pushed back slightly from the table—a blank expression still on his face, save for a slight twinkle in his eyes—turned to Larry Henry, and said laughingly, "And you didn't think I could control my emotions."[62]

"I owe you a drink on that one, 'cause you sure did that time!"[63] Henry chuckled. By now, other people in the room were laughing quietly, relishing the predicament Warden had managed to get himself into and at the same time grateful they didn't have to take the heat.

The mood quickly turned serious. "If they want to fight the war," Horner said, referring to the people in Washington who had helped put Instant Thunder together, "tell them to come to theater. Jimmie Adams knows you don't fight from Washington!"[64] The CENTAF staff murmured their approval. They had heard rumors all week long about some hotshots from Washington who were on their way to the theater with instructions on how to fight the war. Horner didn't like outsiders telling him what to do, especially ivory tower types like John Warden. The last 30 minutes made that perfectly clear.

"Can I have Steve?" asked Horner, casually poking a finger at Foose Wilson.

Warden was in a daze. "Well," he stammered, "I'm not his boss, but I'm sure you can."

"Deptula," growled Horner, "can you stick around?"

"Yes, sir," answered Deptula, who had flown with Horner several years before. "If you want me, I'll be happy to stay and help."

"How about you?" asked Horner, pointing at Ben Harvey, who had been writing furiously, discreetly trying to capture the entire briefing on paper. The lieutenant colonel looked up from his notebook and nodded.

"How about you?" he asked Ron Stanfill. The F-111 pilot broke into a wide grin and gave a thumbs-up.[65]

Horner offered no more invitations. John Warden was going home.

Notes

1. Maj Ronald E. Bergquist, *The Role of Airpower in the Iran-Iraq War* (Maxwell AFB, Ala.: Air University Press, December 1988).
2. Personal notes, Lt Col Dave Deptula. Information extracted here and in subsequent references is unclassified. Hereinafter referred to as Deptula.
3. Ibid.
4. Ibid.
5. Ibid.
6. Ibid.
7. Notes, Lt Col Ben Harvey, 109, Desert Story Collection, US Air Force Historical Research Agency, Maxwell AFB, Ala. (Secret) Information extracted here and in subsequent references is unclassified. Hereinafter referred to as Harvey.
8. Deptula.
9. Col James Crigger, Shaw AFB, S.C., transcript of interviews with Lt Col Suzanne B. Gehri and author, 2–4 December 1991, 16–20, Desert Story Collection, US Air Force Historical Research Agency, Maxwell AFB, Ala.
10. Harvey, 110.
11. Crigger, 2–4 December 1991, 15–17.
12. Harvey, 110.
13. Deptula.
14. Ibid.
15. Col John A. Warden III, Washington, D.C., transcript of interview with Lt Col Suzanne B. Gehri, 22 October 1991, 107, Desert Story Collection, US Air Force Historical Research Agency, Maxwell AFB, Ala.
16. Ibid., 108.
17. Ibid., 107.
18. Deptula.
19. Ibid.
20. Ibid.
21. Ibid.
22. Ibid.
23. Harvey, 116.
24. Ibid., 116–17.
25. Ibid., 117.
26. Ibid.
27. Ibid.
28. Ibid., 117–18.

29. Deptula. For a slightly different version of this exchange between Warden and Horner, see Harvey, 117–20.

30. Harvey, 118.

31. Deptula.

32. Harvey, 118.

33. Ibid.

34. Deptula.

35. Harvey, 119.

36. Deptula.

37. Harvey, 121.

38. Ibid.

39. Deptula.

40. Harvey, 122.

41. Ibid.

42. Ibid.

43. Ibid.

44. Ibid.

45. Ibid., 122–23.

46. Ibid.

47. Ibid.

48. Ibid., 123.

49. Ibid.

50. Ibid., 124.

51. Ibid.

52. Ibid., 125.

53. Ibid.

54. Ibid.

55. Warden, 22 October 1991, 109.

56. Ibid.

57. Ibid.

58. Ibid.

59. Ibid.

60. Ibid.

61. Ibid.

62. Lt Col Dave Deptula, Washington, D.C., transcript of interview with Lt Col Suzanne B. Gehri, Lt Col Edward C. Mann, and author, 23 May 1991, 47, Desert Story Collection, US Air Force Historical Research Agency, Maxwell AFB, Ala.

63. Ibid.

64. Harvey, 125.

65. Deptula.

Epilogue

A bone-weary and thoroughly disheartened John Warden did leave Saudi Arabia the evening of 20 August 1990, but the Instant Thunder plan he had brought to the theater stayed and flourished there. The months ahead would vindicate Warden and his air power ideas in ways even his most ardent supporters would never have dreamt possible. Ironically, it was General Horner's decision not to keep Warden in-theater that allowed the plan to move from a rejected idea to bombs on targets.

Back in Washington, Warden and a contingent of planning, intelligence, and operational personnel—both military and civilian—exploited their connections to high-level federal agencies and routinely provided ideas, suggestions, and critical data to Deptula, Harvey, and Stanfill, who had been left behind in Riyadh and needed all the help they could get. Shuffling from place to place and working with an old Macintosh computer they had scrounged from a supply sergeant who took pity on them, the trio bore no resemblance to the powerful CENTAF planning force that would evolve from their humble beginnings.

Less than 48 hours after Warden's departure, the three lieutenant colonels were joined at RSAF headquarters by Brig Gen Buster C. Glosson, an outspoken, baritone-voiced North Carolinian known for his fiery temper and fighter-pilot get-it-done attitude. Glosson had been languishing on the USS *LaSalle* as part of CENTCOM's "floating staff" when Horner called and asked him to help with the planning effort.[1] He leapt at the chance. From the end of August to the outbreak of the war on 17 January 1991 and its conclusion 42 days later, Glosson became the engine that drove the Desert Storm air campaign.

Not long after the one-star took control of the planning process, it became apparent that he was more comfortable working with Deptula than the other two men. Despite their best intentions, on more than one occasion Harvey and Stanfill found themselves on the outside looking in. Increasingly bitter and frustrated after several weeks in-theater, they returned to the States, where they rejoined Warden in Checkmate and immersed themselves in the task of providing highly sensitive information support to Glosson and Deptula.

The close working relationship and trust that developed between Glosson, Deptula, and Horner not only figured heavily in the survival and expansion of the Instant Thunder plan and the influence of the Checkmate planners on events in Riyadh, but also allowed Deptula to succeed where Warden had failed. He was able to convince both Glosson and Horner of the efficacy of Instant Thunder and the overarching value of strategic attack. His loose, nonthreatening style and seemingly limitless energy appealed to the two senior officers. Simply put, Dave Deptula fit in; John Warden did not.

One of the keys to Deptula's success was his uncanny ability to make difficult things seem easy and bring solutions where others brought only problems. His work depended heavily upon the efforts of the ever-expanding Checkmate team, which swung into 24-hour operations for the duration of the war. The connection with Warden gave Deptula the edge in every aspect of the planning process. As a result, phase one of Horner's air campaign looked remarkably like John Warden's Instant Thunder.

Just as importantly, as the months rolled by and the massive buildup of men and machines created both problems and targeting opportunities for coalition planners, Deptula's rapport with Glosson and Horner allowed Warden and Checkmate to pass critical ideas and information to both men. However, this young lieutenant colonel was no mere conduit for the ideas of John Warden and the Checkmate information mafia. Deptula was an air power thinker and strategist in his own right and exerted tremendous influence on the size and shape of the air campaign. Through Glosson and Horner, he was able to affect what, where, when, and how targets were attacked, disabled, or destroyed. If Glosson was the air campaign's engine, then surely Dave Deptula was the fuel. That, however, is another story.

Note

1. Lt Gen Charles A. Horner, Shaw AFB, S.C., transcript of interview with Lt Col Suzanne B. Gehri and author, 3 December 1991, 15, Desert Story Collection, US Air Force Historical Research Agency, Maxwell AFB, Ala.

What Became of Them?

Adams, Jimmie   Lt Gen, USAF   **Promoted** to general on 13 February 1991; retired as commander of Pacific Air Forces, Hickam AFB, Hawaii, on 1 February 1993.

Alexander, Robert   Maj Gen, USAF   **Promoted** to lieutenant general on 2 August 1991 and became the deputy assistant secretary of defense for military manpower and personnel policy, Office of the Secretary of Defense, Washington, D.C.; now retired.

Autry, Dale   Lt Col, USAF   **Promoted** to colonel; currently an instructor in the Department of Military Studies, Air War College, Maxwell AFB, Alabama.

Baptiste, Sam   Lt Col, USAF   **Promoted** to colonel; currently the director of operations, Southeast Air Defense Sector, Tyndall AFB, Florida.

Bettinger, Alex   Col, USAF   **Retired** in grade.

Bigelow, Dick   Col, USAF   **Retired** in grade.

Blackburn, Jim   Col, USAF   **Retired** in grade.

Boyd, Charles   Lt Gen, USAF   **Promoted** to general on 1 December 1992; now the deputy CINC, United States European Command, Stuttgart, Germany.

Bristow, Rich   Col, USAF   **Worked** on the staff of Air Combat Command, Langley AFB, Virginia; retired in May 1994.

Butler, Lee   Lt Gen, USAF   **Promoted** to general on 25 January 1991; retired as commander of US Strategic

Command, Offutt AFB, Nebraska, on 1 March 1994.

Carns, Mike	Lt Gen, USAF	**Promoted** to general on 16 May 1991; appointed as vice-chief of staff, Headquarters USAF, Washington, D.C.; now retired.
Chain, John	Gen, USAF	**Retired** in grade, 1 February 1991.
Clapper, James	Maj Gen, USAF	**Promoted** to lieutenant general on 15 November 1991; now director of the Defense Intelligence Agency, Washington, D.C.
Crigger, Jim	Col, USAF	**Retired** in grade.
Deptula, Dave	Lt Col, USAF	**Promoted** to colonel; now the Air Force special assistant to the congressionally appointed Military Roles and Missions Commission.
Dugan, Mike	Gen, USAF	**Replaced** as USAF chief of staff on 17 September 1990 by SECDEF Dick Cheney; retired from active duty on 1 January 1991; currently the president of the National Multiple Sclerosis Society.
Glosson, Buster	Brig Gen, USAF	**Promoted** to lieutenant general on 1 June 1993; served as deputy chief of staff for plans and operations, Headquarters USAF, Washington, D.C.; retired 30 June 1994.
Griffith, Tom	Brig Gen, USAF	**Promoted** to lieutenant general on 1 August 1994; currently the commander of Twelfth Air Force/United States Southern Command

		at Davis-Monthan AFB, Arizona.
Harvey, Ben	Lt Col, USAF	**Promoted** to colonel; now the special assistant to the commander of US Southern Command, Quarry Heights, Panama.
Hawkins, Doug	Col, USAF	**Retired** in grade.
Henry, Larry	Brig Gen, USAF	**Promoted** to major general on 1 December 1991; served as deputy chief of plans and operations, Headquarters USAF, Washington, D.C.; now retired.
Horner, Charles	Lt Gen, USAF	**Promoted** to general on 1 July 1992; became CINC of US Space Command, Peterson AFB, Colorado; now retired.
Jeremiah, Dave	Adm, USN	**Served** as vice-chairman of the JCS, Washington, D.C.; now retired.
Johnston, Bob	Maj Gen, USMC	**Promoted** to lieutenant general on 1 October 1991; now deputy chief of staff for manpower and reserve affairs, Headquarters USMC, Washington, D.C.
Kelly, Tom	Lt Gen, USA	**Retired** in grade, 31 March 1991.
Leonardo, John	Col, USAF	**Retired** in grade.
Loh, Mike	Gen, USAF	**Commander,** Air Combat Command, Langley AFB, Virginia.
May, Charles	Maj Gen, USAF	**Promoted** to lieutenant general on 1 February 1991; retired as USAF assistant vice-chief of staff on 1 July 1992.

Meier, Jim	Maj Gen, USAF	**Retired** in grade, 1 January 1993.
Moore, Burton	Maj Gen, USAF	**Retired** in grade, 1 July 1992.
Olsen, Tom	Maj Gen, USAF	**Retired** in grade, 1 November 1991.
Powell, Colin	Gen, USA	**Retired** in grade, 30 September 1993.
Rogers, Buck	Maj, USAF	**Promoted** to lieutenant colonel; now a squadron director of operations, Royal Air Force, Lakenheath, England.
Russ, Robert	Gen, USAF	**Retired** in grade, 1 May 1991.
Ryan, Michael	Maj Gen, USAF	**Promoted** to lieutenant general on 10 May 1993; now commander of 16th Air Force and of Allied Air Forces Southern Europe in Naples, Italy.
Schwarzkopf, H. Norman	Gen, USA	**Retired** in grade, 31 August 1991.
Stanfill, Ron	Lt Col, USAF	**Promoted** to colonel; now a wing vice-commander, Andersen AFB, Guam.
Warden, John	Col, USAF	**Retained** in the grade of colonel; now commandant of Air Command and Staff College, Maxwell AFB, Alabama.
Wilson, Steve	Lt Col, USAF	**Promoted** to colonel; drowned while serving at Kadena AB, Japan, 5 June 1993.

Glossary

AB	air base
ABM	antiballistic missile
ACC	Air Combat Command
ACE	airlift control element
AFB	Air Force base
AFIA	Air Force Intelligence Agency
AMC	Air Mobility Command
AOR	area of responsibility
APC	armored personnel carrier
ATO	air tasking order
ATTG	automated tactical target graphics
AU	Air University
BDU	battle-dress uniform
C^2	command and control
CAP	combat air patrol
CENTAF	US Air Forces, Central Command
CENTCOM	United States Central Command
CHOP	change of operational procedures
CIA	Central Intelligence Agency
CINC	commander in chief
CINCCENT	commander in chief, US Central Command
CINCLANT	commander in chief, US Atlantic Command
CJCS	chairman of the Joint Chiefs of Staff
DACT	dissimilar air combat tactics
DIA	Defense Intelligence Agency
ECM	electronic countermeasures
HQ	headquarters
ICBM	intercontinental ballistic missile
J-3	Operations Directorate
J-4	Logistics Directorate
J-5	Strategic Plans and Policy Directorate
JCS	Joint Chiefs of Staff
JOC	joint operations center
LIMDIS	limited distribution
MAC	Military Airlift Command
NBC	nuclear, biological, and chemical
NCA	national command authorities

NSA	National Security Agency
OPLAN	operational plan
PGM	precision guided munition
PSYOPS	psychological operations
RSAF	Royal Saudi Air Force
SAC	Strategic Air Command
SAM	surface-to-air missile
SAR	special access required
SEAD	suppression of enemy air defenses
SECDEF	secretary of defense
TAC	Tactical Air Command
TACC	tactical air control center
TDY	temporary duty
TLAM	Tomahawk land attack missile
TPFDD	time-phased force deployment data
TPFDL	time-phased force and deployment list
USAF	United States Air Force
USMTM	US Military Training Mission
VOQ	visiting officers' quarters

Index

Bristow, Rich: 39–40, 44–45, 75–77, 82–83, 96–103, 135
Bubiyan Island, Kuwait: 2
Bush, George: 5, 11, 29, 95–96
Butler, Lee: 51–52, 71, 73–74, 78, 80, 135

C-5: 86–89
C-21: 9, 13
C-21A: 89
Cabinet: 10–11
Campaign Plans and Applications Organizations: 35
Camp David: 9–10, 12
Carns, Mike: 71, 79–80, 136
Caruana, Pat: 115
Casualties
civilian: 54, 103
military: 108
CENTAF Rear: 34
Center for Strategic and International Studies: 35
Centers of gravity: 17–18, 72
Central Intelligence Agency (CIA): 10, 33, 93
Chain, John ("Jack"): 25, 27, 35, 136
Chairman of the Joint Chiefs of Staff (CJCS): 56–57, 59, 71–73, 75, 78–79, 81–83, 95, 124, 127
Change of operational procedures (CHOP): 26
Chaos theory: 18
Checkmate Directorate: 16, 18–22, 24–26, 28–30, 33–36, 53, 55, 71, 75–77, 80, 85–86, 96–100, 116, 133–34
Chemical warfare: 11, 24, 56, 115
Cheney, Dick: 1, 9–10, 12–13, 95
Clapper, James R., Jr.: 31–34, 36, 136
Coalition: 52, 103, 108, 122, 124, 134
Cohen, Eliot: 36
Cold war: 16
Collateral damage: 54

Combat
air patrol (CAP): 105
employment: 16
Command and control (C^2): 4–5, 54, 123, 127
Commander in chief (CINC): 1–2, 5–7, 19, 23–24, 47, 53, 56, 74–75, 80–83, 96–97, 101, 103–10, 121, 126
Central Command (CINCCENT): 74
United States Atlantic Command (CINCLANT): 26
Communications: 19, 34, 39, 49, 54
Concept of operations: 15, 54, 105
Congress: 2
Contingencies: 4, 16, 20
Counterair: 32
Crigger, Jim: 3, 90, 115–17, 122, 124, 136

D day: 116–17
Deception plan: 52, 109, 114
Defense Intelligence Agency (DIA): 1, 33, 93
Defensive plan: 10, 90, 116–17, 125–27
Deployment: 5–7, 15, 20–21, 32, 34–35, 39, 55, 58, 95, 106, 109, 121, 125
Deptula, Dave: 21–22, 28, 35, 85–86, 92, 97, 113–21, 128–29, 133–34, 136
Desert: 54, 85, 114, 127
Dhahran, Saudi Arabia: 88
Dissimilar air combat tactics (DACT): 3
Doctrine, aerospace/Air Force: 22, 48, 108, 117
Douhet, [Giulio]: 40
Dover AFB, Delaware: 86, 89
Dugan, Mike: 16, 23, 26–27, 30, 35, 50–51, 81, 106, 110, 136
Dunn, Mike: 15–16

Eckberg, Jim: 21

National
command authorities (NCA): 16
objectives: 28
paralysis: 103, 108
Security Agency (NSA): 33
Night strike: 124
Ninth Air Force: 3, 20, 25, 32–34, 97, 99–100, 116
Nuclear, biological, and chemical (NBC): 42, 54
Nuclear targeting: 92

Oil, Saudi: 116
Olsen, Tom: 90–91, 115–19, 121–22, 137
Operation
Desert Shield/Storm: 97, 133
plan (OPLAN): 3, 6, 20, 114, 125
Operations, military: 3, 19, 33, 58, 73–74, 79, 105–6, 115–16, 119–20, 122, 125, 133

Patrick AFB, Florida: 77–78
Patriot missile: 11
Patton, [George]: 58
Pentagon: 1, 9, 13, 15–16, 19–20, 22, 25, 31, 33–34, 39, 45, 47, 49, 71, 75, 77–80, 82, 84, 86, 89–90, 95, 98–99, 101, 113, 120
Persian
Gulf: 13, 21, 33, 95, 107
Gulf battle group: 118
Peters, Tom: 18
Planners, military: 6, 8, 25–27, 34, 42–43, 45, 51, 53, 55–56, 58, 71, 74, 79, 98–99, 113, 115, 118, 123, 134
Planning, military (esp. Instant Thunder): 8, 13, 16, 25, 28–29, 33, 35–36, 42, 47, 56–58, 75–76, 78, 80, 84, 96–97, 106, 108, 116–18, 125–28, 133–34
Population, civilian: 17–18, 54
Powell, Colin: 1, 9, 11, 13, 23, 25, 35, 59, 71–74, 80–82, 95, 102, 106, 121, 137

Precision guided munitions (PGM): 21, 36
Preemptive attack: 102
Presidential objectives: 29, 53
President [of the United States]: 2, 4, 9–13, 42, 56, 73, 93, 95–96, 102
Press, American: 44
Psychological operations (PSYOPS): 54, 105
Public, American: 44–45
Purple
suiters: 20
water fountain: 16, 80

Qadhafi, Muammar: 125

Ramstein AB, Germany: 87
Rand Corporation: 36
RC-135: 113
Reconnaissance: 16, 114
Red Sea task force: 118
Regional conflicts: 102
Republican Guard: 72
Reserve forces: 20
Rice, Donald B.: 21–22, 28
Rider, Bill: 13
Riyadh, Saudi Arabia: 39, 41, 43, 75, 85–86, 89, 107, 110, 113–16, 118–21, 123, 133–34
Rogers, Gen Buck: 53, 55–58, 108–9
Rogers, Maj Buck: 114, 137
Role of Airpower in the Iran-Iraq War, The: 113
Rolling Thunder: 29
Route packages: 117, 124
Royal Saudi Air Force (RSAF): 89, 91, 93, 115, 119–21, 133
Run-in lines: 97–98
Russ, Robert D.: 23, 25–27, 34–35, 39–45, 49–51, 75–77, 81, 100, 102, 117, 138
Ryan, Michael ("Mike"): 34, 41, 45, 47–49, 96–97, 99, 138

Saudi Arabia: 4, 9, 11–13, 20, 39–40, 42, 55–56, 75, 81, 89–90,

92, 97, 100, 106–7, 109, 114,
116–17, 119, 125, 127, 133
Schlieffen
Alfred von: 105
Plan: 105–6
Schwarzkopf, H. Norman: 1–13,
23–28, 31–32, 35–36, 47, 49–59,
71, 74, 79, 81, 90, 92, 97–98,
101, 103–10, 119, 121, 125, 138
Scud missiles: 11, 24, 107–8
Sea power: 20, 54
2d Armored Division: 125
Secretary
of the Air Force: 21
of defense (SECDEF): 1, 9–10,
12, 74
of state: 11–12
Selective bombing: 40
Sewell, Tom: 6
Shaw AFB, South Carolina: 2–4,
12–13, 33–34, 97
Sorties: 124
Southwest Asia: 18
Soviet Union: 16
Special
access required (SAR): 86
operations: 98, 114
Stanfill, Ron: 51, 81, 113–16,
118–19, 121, 125, 128, 130,
133, 138
State Department: 121
Strategic
air campaign: 10–11, 17, 22,
24–25, 27–28, 31–32, 34, 41,
45, 53, 55, 71, 73–75, 79,
81–82, 90–92, 96, 98, 103–4,
120, 128, 133–34
Air Command (SAC): 19, 24, 27,
35–36, 96, 98
objectives: 48
Strike package configuration: 41
Suppression of enemy air defenses
(SEAD): 41, 105, 108–9
Surface-to-air missiles (SAM): 109
Surface-to-surface missiles: 107
Suter, Moody: 16

System specialists: 35

TAC alternative plan: 40, 42–45,
48, 102
Tactical
Air Command (TAC): 24–25,
34–36, 39, 43, 47–51, 57, 75–77,
81, 96–102, 117
air control center (TACC): 97,
119
Tactical/strategic warfare: 124,
134
Tanker aircraft: 7, 16, 24, 35, 74,
82, 107
Tank (secure area): 1, 95
Tel Aviv, Israel: 107
Tenth Air Force: 34
Third Army: 11
36th Tactical Fighter Wing: 113
*Thriving on Chaos: Handbook for a
Management Revolution*: 18
Tiger team: 16, 19
Time-phased force deployment
data (TPFDD): 5
list (TPFDL): 20
Timing: 115
Tomahawk land attack missile
(TLAM): 97, 104, 123–24
Turkey: 57, 106

United Nations Security Council:
109
United States: 11, 15–16, 29,
41–42, 44–45, 54, 92, 110,
121–22, 133
US
aircraft: 8, 11, 20–21, 34, 52,
55, 90, 106, 108, 117–18, 127
Air Force: 1–2, 15–16, 20,
23–24, 27–28, 31, 34, 39–40,
43–44, 48–49, 52, 56, 71,
74–75, 79–81, 84, 87, 115,
117–18, 121
Air Forces, Central Command
(CENTAF): 6, 9, 34, 36, 39, 56,
90–92, 114–22, 124–25, 129, 133